SUMMER SKILLS for the 2nd Grade Graduate

Written by Cynthia Benjamin

Annotated Bibliography provided by Sara Freeman

Illustrated by Jim Connolly

Senior Editor: Christine Hood
Editor: Concetta Doti Ryan, M.A.
Inside Design: Rose Sheifer
Cover Design: Joanne Caroselli
Cover Photography: ©1998 Comstock, Inc.

Frank Schaffer Publications
23740 Hawthorne Blvd.
Torrance, CA 90505

© 1998 Frank Schaffer Publications. All rights reserved. Printed in the United States of America.

Notice! Pages may be reproduced for classroom or home use only, not for commercial resale. No part of this publication may be reproduced for storage in a retrieval system, or transmitted in any form or by any means—electronic, mechanical, recording, etc.—without the prior written permission of the publisher. Reproduction of these materials for an entire school or school system is strictly prohibited.

Table of Contents

Parent Letter 4

Making the Most of "Summer Skills" 5

Fun Everyday Learning Activities . . . 8

Reading Favorites Children Love 9

Week 1 13
- Language Arts
  (phonics, vocabulary, categorizing, parts of speech)
- Math
  (addition, subtraction, patterns, multiplication)

Week 2 21
- Language Arts
  (synonyms & antonyms, picture clues, phonics, compound words, vowel sounds)
- Math
  (patterns, fractions, telling time)

Week 3 29
- Language Arts
  (drawing conclusions, punctuation, plurals, contractions)
- Math
  (addition, subtraction, telling time, measurement, multiplication)

Week 4 37
- Language Arts
  (punctuation, capitalization, phonics, alphabetizing, sequencing)
- Math
  (fractions, measurement, patterns)

Week 5 45
- Language Arts
  (context clues, categorizing, syllables, rhyming words, plurals)
- Math
  (money, word problems, place value)

Week 6 53
- Language Arts
  (comprehension, parts of speech)
- Math
  (money, addition, subtraction, multiplication, numerical order)

Week 7 61
- Language Arts
  (sequencing, phonics, alphabetizing, blends)
- Math
  (numerical order, word problems, telling time, odd & even numbers)

Week 8 69
- Language Arts
  (syllables, capitalization, comprehension, verb tense)
- Math
  (place value, subtraction, telling time, word problems)

Week 9 77
- Language Arts
  (parts of speech, capitalization, punctuation, apostrophes, phonics)
- Math
  (graphing, addition, place value, word problems)

Week 10 85
- Language Arts
  (homonyms, letter writing, story writing)
- Math
  (greater than/less than, addition, subtraction, fractions, word problems)

Certificate of Completion 93

Answer Key 94

Assessment Overview 97

Flash Cards and Charts 105

Dear Parents,

Congratulations! Your choice of this book shows that you are concerned about the education and development of your child. You are willing to go that extra mile to ensure that your child continues to grow and learn over the summer months. Although he or she learns a lot in school, you are your child's most important teacher. Showing your child how important learning is to you will motivate him or her by your example.

Summer vacation is a time for rest, renewal, and good old fun! You want to make sure, however, that your child continues to grow academically during the time he or she is away from the classroom. Ten weeks away from school is a long time, but this time can be used productively to reinforce and maintain the skills your child has worked so hard to learn during the school year. Second grade is an incredibly important year in a child's education. Basic reading, writing, and math skills have been developed, and daily practice in these areas is the key to continued success.

Summer Skills for the 2nd Grade Graduate is designed to keep your child's reading, writing, and math skills honed during the summer months. This book isn't designed as a typical textbook. Instead, it offers a series of fun, engaging activities that will delight, challenge, and motivate your child to keep learning as he or she practices essential math, reading, and language arts skills taught in the second grade. When September comes, your child will be ready to leap into third grade!

Show your child that learning is an everyday experience, one that can be fun, adventurous, and challenging. "Take a bow" for demonstrating that you value education and for lending a hand toward the goal of lifetime learning for your child. Best of all, you will be doing it together! Nothing delights your child more than individual attention from his or her favorite adult—you! Your involvement as a partner in your child's education is something to be proud of. So, enjoy the summer, and better yet, enjoy spending this treasured time helping your child learn.

Making the Most of "Summer Skills"

Summer Skills for the 2nd Grade Graduate provides an important link between your child's second- and third-grade school year. It reviews what your child learned in the second grade, providing the confidence and skills that he or she needs for the coming fall. The activities in this book will help your child successfully bridge the gap between second and third grade by reviewing and reinforcing the important and essential skills for his or her continued academic success. These activities are designed to

- review skills in math, reading, and language arts that second graders learned the previous year.
- give you an opportunity to monitor your child's skills in various areas.
- offer you a chance to spend special time with your child.
- enable your child to continue routine daily learning activities.
- give you a chance to praise your child's efforts.
- demonstrate to your child that you value lifetime learning.
- make you an active and important part of your child's educational development.

About the Book

This resource contains a myriad of fun and challenging reading, writing, and math activities. The reading and writing pages provide practice in reading comprehension, compound words, grammar, spelling, phonics, and writing. The math pages review skills taught in second grade, such as basic addition and subtraction, as well as regrouping, writing numerals, patterning, place value, telling time, and story problems. The pages at the end of the book include flash cards and charts that reinforce basic skills. These can be torn out and used for practice again and again.

Most of the activities in the book are designed so that your child can work independently. However, your child will enjoy the activities much more if you work alongside him or her. Make sure to let your child know that this is not a workbook with tests, but a book of fun activities that you can do together. The book is divided into ten weeks, with approximately eight activity pages per week. These activities are divided between math and language arts. Feel free to choose how many per day and in which order you do the activities, but complete the weeks in sequence, since activities become increasingly challenging as the book progresses. The end of the book features ideas on assessing your child's progress throughout the summer. The tests included in the section focus on the same skills that are highlighted in the book's activities and will help familiarize your child with various testing formats.

Also included in the book is a Certificate of Completion (page 93). Give this to your child at the end of the summer or when he or she has completed all of the activities in the book. Invite him or her to color the certificate, and then frame it for the whole family to admire. Your child will feel a proud sense of accomplishment.

Getting Started

In order for your child to get the most from the activities in this resource, use these helpful tips to make these learning experiences interesting and, most of all, fun!

- Set aside a time each day for completing the activities. Make it a time when your child will be most ready to learn, and make it a routine.
- Provide a pleasant, quiet place to work. This means no television or radio in your child's work area. Also make sure there is a sufficient light source.
- Review in advance the activity page(s) your child will complete that session. This way you will be able to familiarize yourself with the lesson as well as what materials will be needed to complete it (e.g., pencil, paper, crayons, scissors). Materials are noted in the upper right-hand corner of each activity page.
- Have your child read directions aloud beforehand to make sure he or she understands the activity. Instructions are written for the child, but he or she may need your help reading and/or understanding them.
- Let your child help choose which activity of the week he or she would like to complete that day.
- Feel free to reward your child for good effort, but avoid bribing him or her into completing activities.
- Praise all your child's work. It's the effort, not necessarily the end result, that counts most.

Using the Flash Cards

The 40 double-sided flash cards at the back of the book are on perforated card stock. They are easily removed, and are sturdy enough to be used again and again. The second-grade book includes flash cards covering basic addition, subtraction, multiplication, and division skills, as well as practice with fractions, telling time, and compound words. Flash cards can be used in a variety of creative and challenging ways:

- Practice sentence making. Have your child choose a word card, then make up a sentence that contains the word.
- Build a "flash-card jail." Have your child sit on the floor and surround him- or herself with the cards. The only way for your child to "escape" is to answer each card correctly.
- Invite your child to race the clock by answering each flash card within a certain time limit. See if he or she can get faster every time!
- Post flash cards all over the house. For example, invite your child to say the answer to a flash card posted on the refrigerator before opening it.

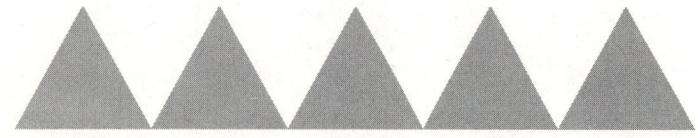

- Hide the cards outside for a "treasure hunt." With each correct answer, give your child a small treat.

- Play a game of "Concentration." Make copies of the cards so you have two of each. Lay the cards face down and draw two. If both of your cards have the same answer you get to keep the pair!

- Hold a card in your hand and give your partner clues until he or she guesses the problem or word you are holding.

- Play a "travel game." First, place ten cards in a row on the floor or table. The first card is the starting point and the last card is the city or country of final destination. Your child must "travel" along this "route" by reading and answering the flash cards correctly. An incorrect answer means your child must place that card back and start over again. The goal is to finish all ten flash cards without stopping. When your child has mastered the first ten cards, move on to the next ten, and so on.

No one knows better than you how your child learns best, so use this book to enhance the way you already work with him or her. Use every opportunity possible as a learning experience, whether making a trip through the grocery store or riding in the car. Pose problems and let your child figure out how to solve them, asking questions such as *Which route should we take to the park? What could we use to make a plant grow straight? How high should we hang this shelf? What color paint best matches our couch?* Also, respond excitedly to discoveries your child makes throughout the day, such as *That rock is really unique! I wonder how long it took the spider to spin that web;* or *You spent your money wisely.* In this way you will encourage and motivate your child to learn throughout the day and for the rest of his or her life, providing the confidence and self-esteem he or she needs for continued academic success.

Fun Everyday Learning Activities

Use these simple educational activities to keep your child's mind engaged and active during the summer months and all year long!

Reading and Language Arts

- Ask your child to make a schedule of events for the day, in the order in which they will take place. Ask him or her to prioritize the list and number the events.
- On a neighborhood walk or while driving in the car, encourage your child to read all the street signs and numbers.
- Read with your child each day. Encourage your child to retell the story to you. Then have him or her make up original adventures for the story characters or write an additional chapter.
- Have your child write down important dates such as family birthdays, important trips or outings, or holidays. Be sure your child capitalizes the name of the month and week and uses a comma between the day and the year.
- During a visit to the park or playground invite your child to describe what he or she sees there using as many adjectives as possible.
- Have your child list three things you can smell, feel, taste, or see in a particular room of the house or on a "senses walk."
- Have your child plan a menu for a meal and write out a grocery list.
- With your child, identify as many opposites in your house or neighborhood as possible. For example, a big car and a small bike; a tall tree and a short bush.
- Take a trip to the zoo, and bring your camera. Take pictures of your child's favorite animals. When you get home, have your child write about each animal, and add the photos. Bind the pages into a zoo book!

Math and Science

- Have your child identify as many parts of the human body as he or she can. Ask him or her to describe the function of each part, if possible.
- Ask your child to read a recipe with you for a simple dish. Practice measuring skills by simulating measuring out the ingredients with water or rice in measuring spoons and cups.
- Encourage your child to read a clock face or a digital clock whenever possible. As an extension, invite your child to tell you what time of day he or she gets up in the morning, eats lunch, feeds the dog, helps around the house, and so on.
- Have your child read the price of items in a store or supermarket. Challenge him or her to estimate how much can be bought with a designated amount of money. Can your child figure out how much change is left over?
- Encourage your child to tell you whether certain objects in your home (sofa, pencil) would be measured in pounds or ounces.
- Fill a measuring cup with water to different levels, and invite your child to read the measurement and then write it as a fraction.
- Ask your child to describe the weather on a particular day, and then guess the temperature.
- Encourage your child to read nonfiction library books and make up creative stories about the subject matter (e.g, lions or airplanes).

Reading Favorites Children Love

Picture Books

Aekyung's Dream by Min Paek (Children's Book Press, rev. ed. 1988). A Korean immigrant girl finds strength through her own heritage in order to adjust to her new life in this tale told in Korean and English.

Annie and the Old One by Miska Miles (Little, Brown, 1971). In this tender tale, a young Navajo girl learns to accept the upcoming death of her grandmother.

Arthur Writes a Story by Marc Brown (Little, Brown, 1996). Young writers will appreciate Arthur's efforts as he tries to improve his story by listening to everyone's input, but he loses his own story in the meantime.

Cloudy With a Chance of Meatballs by Judi Barrett (Atheneum, 1978). The weather is really wacky in this story of the land of Chewandswallow.

Cross-Country Cat by Mary Calhoun (Morrow, 1979). When a cat gets left behind at a cabin, it manages to cross-country ski back to its owners. Look for other adventures by Calhoun about this clever cat.

The Doorbell Rang by Pat Hutchins (Greenwillow, 1986). In this amusing story, every time a pair of children gets ready to eat a dozen cookies, the doorbell rings, more children arrive, and the cookies need to be redivided.

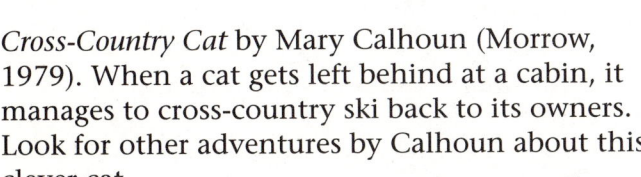

The Elephant's Child by Rudyard Kipling (Harcourt Brace, 1983). This wonderfully illustrated version by Lorinda Bryan Cauley captures the humor of Kipling's tale of how the elephant got its trunk.

Hershel and the Hanukkah Goblins by Eric A. Kimmel (Holiday House, 1989). Hershel of Ostropol outwits silly and scary goblins, thus enabling a village to celebrate Hanukkah.

Horton Hatches the Egg by Dr. Seuss (Random House, 1940). A faithful elephant cares for the nest of a lazy bird in this whimsical story told in verse.

Maria Molina and the Days of the Dead by Kathleen Krull (Macmillan, 1994). A girl and her family celebrate this Mexican holiday of remembrance.

Nine O'Clock Lullaby by Marilyn Singer (HarperCollins, 1991). While a child listens to a bedtime story in Brooklyn, other children around the world are busy doing different things, depending on the time.

Something Queer Is Going On (A Mystery) by Elizabeth Levy (Delacorte, 1973). Best friends Jill and Gwen solve the mysterious kidnapping of Jill's dog in this first volume of a delightful series.

Storm in the Night by Mary Stolz (HarperCollins, 1988). In this warm family tale, a grandfather shares stories with his grandson when the lights go out in a storm.

The True Story of the 3 Little Pigs! by Jon Scieszka (Viking, 1989). The humorous retelling of the classic folktale from Alexander T. Wolf's point of view.

The Wave of the Sea Wolf by David Wisniewski (Clarion, 1994). Intricate cut-paper illustrations will fascinate readers in this story of a Tlingit girl who receives a gift from the Sea-Wolf.

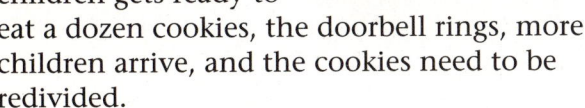

Easy Readers

Amelia Bedelia by Peggy Parish (HarperCollins, 1963). A maid who takes her directions very literally is the star of this funny series.

The Josefina Story Quilt by Eleanor Coerr (HarperCollins, 1986). A young girl does not want to give up her hen in this wagon-train adventure.

Keep the Lights Burning, Abbie by Peter and Connie Roop (Carolrhoda, 1985). This is the true story of a girl in 1856 who keeps the lighthouse lamps lit during a winter storm.

My Brother, Ant by Betsy Byars (Viking, 1996). The adventures of two brothers are told in four chapters.

Nate the Great and the Fishy Prize by Marjorie Weinman Sharmat (Coward-McCann, 1985). This is one in a series of books about Nate the Great—a boy detective.

Pinky and Rex by James Howe (Atheneum, 1990). Pinky is a boy and Rex is a girl, and they are the best of friends. Look for other volumes of this beginning chapter book series.

Sleeping Ugly by Jane Yolen (Coward-McCann, 1981). Mean but beautiful Princess Miserella and kind Plain Jane both get what they deserve in this satisfying fairy tale.

Wagon Wheels by Barbara Brenner (HarperCollins, rev. ed. 1993). This is the poignant tale of an African American pioneer family.

Young Harriet Tubman: Freedom Fighter by Anne Benjamin (Troll, 1992). This biography features the heroine who helped more than 300 slaves escape to freedom.

Chapter Books

Bunnicula by Deborah and James Howe (Atheneum, 1979). When a strange rabbit joins a household, the family cat and dog become convinced it's a vampire bunny.

The Cat's Meow by Gary Soto (Scholastic, 1995). Graciela can't believe her ears when her cat Pip begins speaking Spanish!

The Cuckoo Child by Dick King-Smith (Hyperion, 1993). An eight-year-old boy who loves birds gets his pet geese to help him raise an ostrich in this funny tale.

Girls to the Rescue: Tales of Clever, Courageous Girls from Around the World selected by Bruce Lansky (Meadowbrook Press, 1995). The title sums up this great collection of stories.

The Hundred Dresses by Eleanor Estes (Harcourt, 1944). A poor girl who claims to have 100 dresses is teased by classmates in this poignant tale of childhood cruelty.

The Iron Giant: A Story in Five Nights by Ted Hughes (Harper, rev. ed. 1988). A fearsome robot stalks the land, but later becomes a hero when he triumphs over an alien.

Mush: A Dog from Space by Daniel Pinkwater (Atheneum, 1995). A girl who has wanted a pet for a long time gets a great one from outer space.

The Real Thief by William Steig (Farrar, Straus, Giroux, 1973). Gawain the goose is unjustly convicted of a crime while the real thief is tortured by his guilty conscience in this thought-provoking animal fantasy.

Winnie-the-Pooh by A. A. Milne (Dutton, 1926). The adventures of Pooh Bear continue to delight listeners—young and old.

Folklore

Adopted by the Eagles by Paul Goble (Bradbury, 1994). Striking illustrations help tell this Lakota tale of friendship and treachery.

The Chinese Mirror by Mirra Ginsburg (Harcourt Brace Jovanovich, 1988). This is a humorous Korean tale of a mirror brought back from China and the trouble it causes.

The Legend of the Poinsettia by Tomie dePaola (Putnam, 1994). This Mexican folktale explains how the poinsettia flower, a symbol of Christmas, came to be.

Llama and the Great Flood by Ellen Alexander (Crowell, 1989). In this Peruvian folktale, a llama dreams of a flood and helps save his owner's family and many other animals who climb to the top of a mountain.

The Mud Pony by Caron Lee Cohen (Scholastic, 1988). This is a Pawnee folktale of a boy whose toy mud pony comes to life and helps him become strong.

Papa Gatto: An Italian Fairy Tale by Ruth Sanderson (Little, Brown, 1995). Elegant illustrations complement this tale of Papa Gatto, cat adviser to the prince, who needs someone to care for his kittens.

The Rough-Face Girl by Rafe Martin (Putnam, 1992). This is an Algonquin version of Cinderella. Compare it to these other Cinderella stories from around the world: *Ashpet, The Egyptian Cinderella, The Irish Cinderlad, Jouanah, Kongi and Potgi, Princess Furball,* and *Yeh-Shen.*

The Stinky Cheese Man and Other Fairly Stupid Tales by Jon Scieszka (Viking, 1992). This book includes a madcap collection of stories such as "The Really Ugly Duckling."

The Tale of Ali Baba and the Forty Thieves by Eric A. Kimmel (Holiday House, 1996). Enchanting illustrations accompany this famous tale from the Arabian Nights.

The Talking Eggs by Robert D. San Souci (Dial, 1989). In this story from the American South, two sisters react very differently when they meet an old woman in the woods, and are rewarded accordingly.

Twelve Tales by Aesop by Eric Carle (Philomel, 1980). Brightly-colored illustrations perfectly match these well-known fables.

Who's in Rabbit's House? by Verna Aardema (Dial, 1977). In this Masai tale, Rabbit enlists the help of many friends to rid her house of the mysterious Long One.

Poetry

Falling Up by Shel Silverstein (HarperCollins, 1996). This is Silverstein's third volume of zany poems and drawings for kids.

For the Love of the Game: Michael Jordan and Me by Eloise Greenfield (HarperCollins, 1997). In this beautifully illustrated picture-book poem, two children discover the importance of their desire and spirit, and recognize their parallels to Michael Jordan.

Hailstones and Halibut Bones by Mary O'Neill (Doubleday, 1961). This collection of color poems, such as "What Is Purple?," makes one think about the colors of words, feelings, and objects all around.

If I Were in Charge of the World and Other Worries by Judith Viorst (Atheneum, 1981). These are great poems for children and their parents to share together.

The Random House Book of Poetry for Children selected by Jack Prelutsky (Random House, 1983). This is an outstanding collection of both fun and serious poems on a variety of topics.

Informational Books

Alvin Ailey by Andrea Davis Pinkney and Brian Pinkney (Hyperion, 1993). This is an illustrated biography of the famed dancer and choreographer. Look for other outstanding biographies by the Pinkneys on Bill Pickett and Benjamin Banneker.

Children Just Like Me by Susan Elizabeth Copsey (Dorling Kindersley, 1995). Color photographs of children, families, schools, toys, food, clothing, and homes help show how children look and live around the world.

The Cloud Book by Tomie dePaola (Holiday House, 1975). This is a fun and friendly book about clouds.

Dinosaurs, Beware! by Marc Brown and Stephen Krensky (Atlantic Monthly, 1982). Humorous illustrations of dinosaurs help teach sixty different safety tips.

Each Orange Had Eight Slices by Paul Giganti Jr. (Greenwillow, 1992). This counting book can be used by second graders as a wonderful introduction to multiplication.

Eleanor by Barbara Cooney (Viking, 1996). Eleanor Roosevelt's difficult childhood is presented in this lovely picture book.

Getting to Know the World's Greatest Composers: Leonard Bernstein by Mike Venezia (Children's Press, 1997). Photographs, cartoons, and simple text make this a fun and informative series.

Glow-in-the-Dark Constellations by C. E. Thompson (Grosset & Dunlap, 1989). Stories and glow-in-the-dark star maps make up this enjoyable reference.

If You Made a Million by David M. Schwartz (Lothrop, 1989). This spirited money book explains coins, paper currency, and checks, ranging from 1¢ to a million dollars.

Magic School Bus Inside the Earth by Joanna Cole (Scholastic, 1987). In this volume of a wacky and fact-filled science series, Ms. Frizzle's class takes a field trip all the way to Earth's core and lives to tell about it.

Many Luscious Lollipops by Ruth Heller (Grosset & Dunlap, 1989). Rhyming verse and colorful illustrations merge in this language picture book about adjectives.

Rosie: A Visiting Dog's Story by Stephanie Calmenson (Houghton Mifflin, 1994). Large color photographs and friendly text explain the moving work of Rosie—a dog who visits hospitals, nursing homes, and schools.

Sarah Morton's Day by Kate Waters (Scholastic, 1989). Photographed at a living history museum, this captivating book details a day in the life of a pilgrim girl. Look for these companion books that relate to a pilgrim boy and a Wampanoag boy: *Samuel Eaton's Day* and *Tapenum's Day*.

The Sioux by Virginia Driving Hawk Sneve (Holiday House, 1993). Beautiful paintings enhance this beginning book that features a creation myth, history, everyday life, and information about the Sioux today. This is part of a series which includes *The Iroquois, The Nez Perce, The Hopis,* and more.

The Story of the Statue of Liberty by Betty and Giulio Maestro (Lothrop, 1986). This picture book describes the history and creation of one of the world's great symbols of freedom.

The Ultimate Bug Book by Luise Woelflein (Artists & Writers Guild, 1993). Pop-ups make learning about insects a treat.

Sound Off

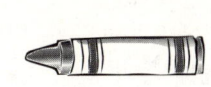

Phonics

Read the words in each row. Circle the words that have the same beginning sound with blue crayon.

1. can   cat   glass   cot   boot

2. pear   hoop   pin   swing   pet

3. bring   dog   broil   drill   bridge

4. frog   trick   star   stair   stage

5. mug   mat   nut   mitt   open

Word Puzzler

Look at the scrambled letters. Then read the meaning of the word. Unscramble the letters to spell the word and write it on the line. The first one is done for you.

1. T-G-I-E-R   Name a striped wild animal. _____tiger_____

2. R-O-N-T-F   What is the opposite of back? _____

3. O-B-K-O   Name something you read. _____

4. G-I-N-S-W   Name something on a playground that moves back and forth. _____

5. A-C-K-J-T-E   Name something you wear outside when it is cold. _____

6. W-I-M-S   What do you do in a pool? _____

7. H-O-S-L-O-C   Name the place you go to learn. _____

8. P-P-L-E-U-R   The name of a color. _____

A Bunch of Balloons

Week 1 — Addition, subtraction

Add or subtract to find the answers. Then color the balloons following the Color Key.

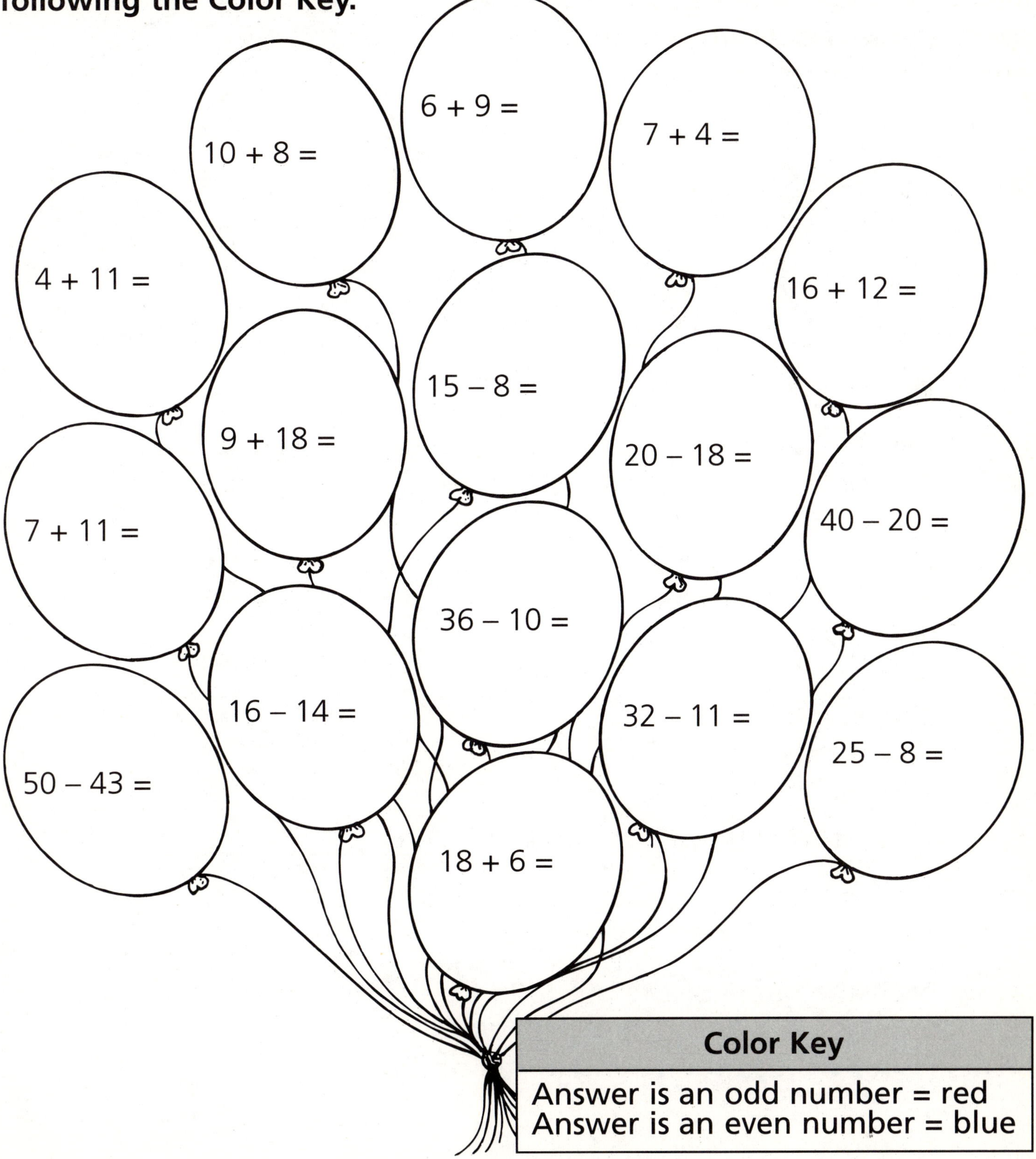

- 10 + 8 =
- 6 + 9 =
- 7 + 4 =
- 4 + 11 =
- 16 + 12 =
- 9 + 18 =
- 15 − 8 =
- 20 − 18 =
- 7 + 11 =
- 40 − 20 =
- 36 − 10 =
- 16 − 14 =
- 32 − 11 =
- 25 − 8 =
- 50 − 43 =
- 18 + 6 =

Color Key

Answer is an odd number = red
Answer is an even number = blue

Word Wheels

Categorizing

Read the group of words on each wheel. In the center of the wheel, write the name for each group. The first one is done for you.

Sample Word Wheel

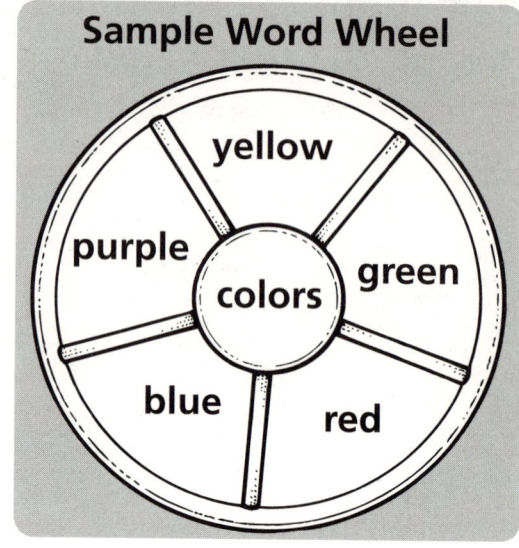

1.

2.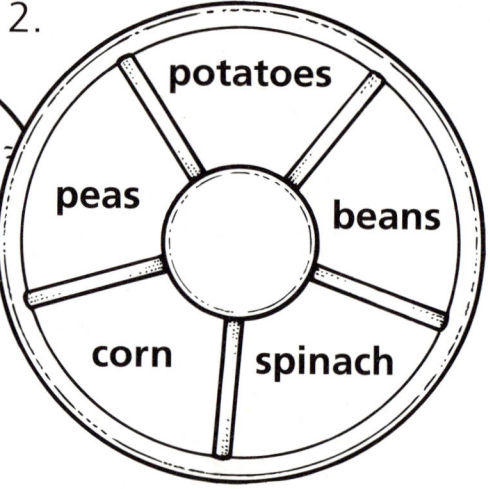

3.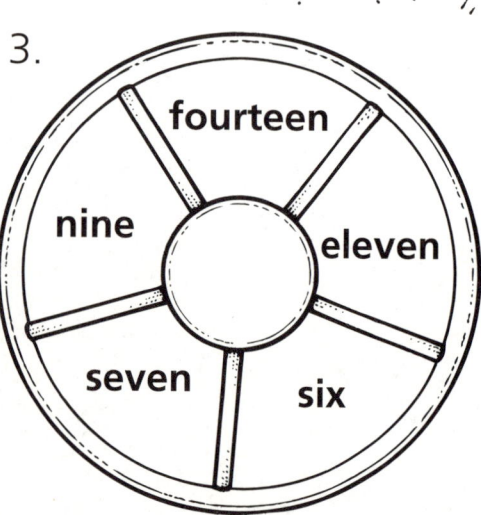

4.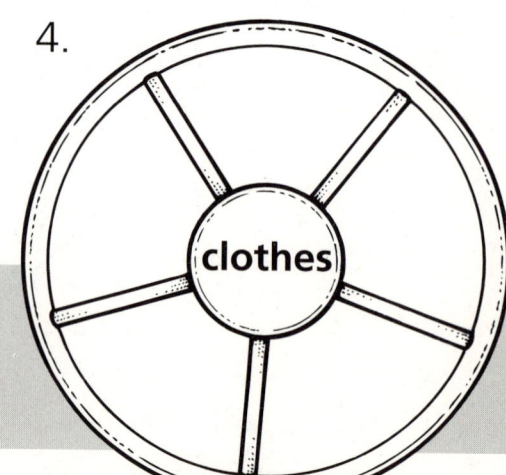

Now, read the name of the group in the center of the wheel. Complete the word wheel with words that belong in the group.

Word Detective

Parts of speech

Look carefully at the picture on this page. In the first column, list ten nouns you see in the picture. In the second column, write the first adjective you think of that describes the noun. The first one is done for you. When you are finished, color the picture.

NOUNS	ADJECTIVES
1. lion	strong
2. _____	_____
3. _____	_____
4. _____	_____
5. _____	_____
6. _____	_____
7. _____	_____
8. _____	_____
9. _____	_____
10. _____	_____

What's Missing?

Patterns

Look at each number pattern. Write the missing numbers on the lines.

1. 2   4   6   8   ___   12   14   16   ___   ___

2. 1   3   5   ___   9   11   13   ___

3. 5   10   ___   20   25   ___   35

4. 12   10   ___   6   4   ___   0

5. 18   ___   12   9   ___   3   0

6. 3   3   6   6   9   ___   12   12   ___   ___

7. 4   8   12   ___   20   ___   28   ___   36

8. ___   18   15   12   ___   ___   ___   0

9. 4   ___   8   8   ___   ___   16   ___   ___

Bunny Trouble

Week 1 — Parts of speech

Help this lost rabbit find his way home across the field. Use a crayon to follow the path of verbs. Be careful or the rabbit won't get home in time for dinner!

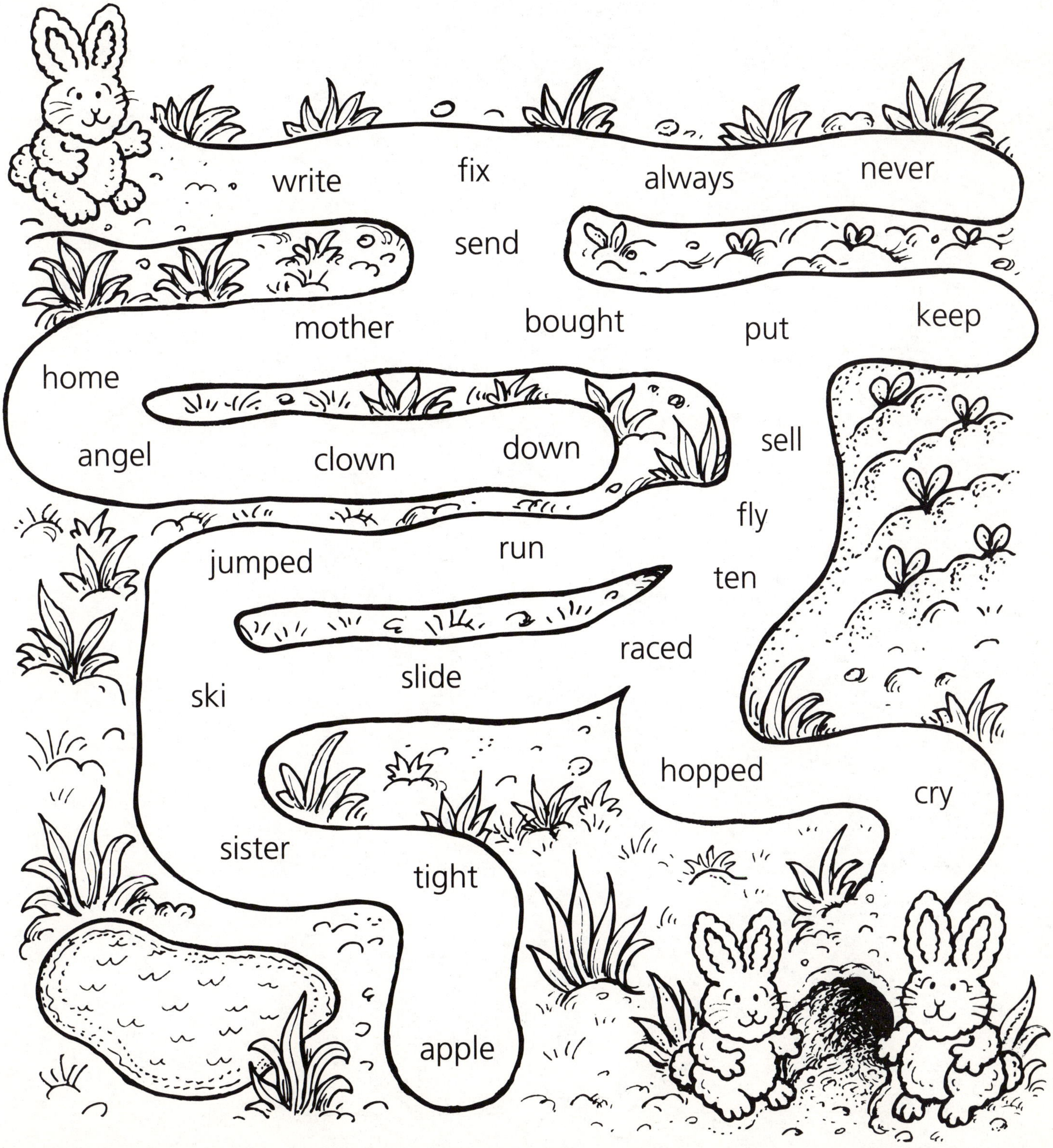

write fix always never
send
mother bought put keep
home
angel clown down sell
fly
jumped run ten
raced
ski slide
hopped cry
sister tight
apple

How Many Suns?

Week 1 — Multiplication

Look at the example below. Then circle each group of suns, write the matching number sentence, and multiply to find the answer.

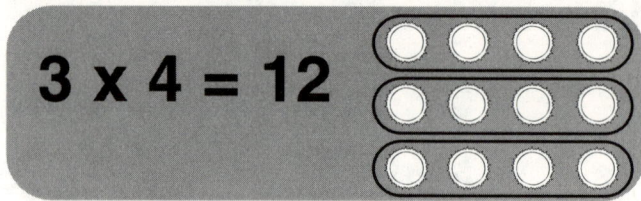
3 x 4 = 12

1. (3 rows of 5)

____ x ____ = ____

2. (3 rows of 7)

____ x ____ = ____

3. (4 rows of 4)

____ x ____ = ____

4. (3 rows of 2)

____ x ____ = ____

5. (2 rows of 5)

____ x ____ = ____

6. (1 row of 5)

____ x ____ = ____

7. (3 rows of 5)

____ x ____ = ____

8. (4 rows of 5)

____ x ____ = ____

Same or Different?

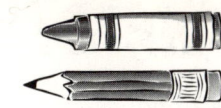 **week 2**
Synonyms & antonyms

Read the words in each line. With red crayon, circle the words with the same meaning.

1.	happy	soft	glad
2.	big	small	huge
3.	smiling	sick	ill
4.	evening	night	sun
5.	chore	job	chart

Read the words in each line. With blue crayon, circle the words with opposite meanings.

6.	hot	long	cold
7.	tall	silly	short
8.	big	quiet	noisy
9.	dark	light	black
10.	merry	sad	happy

Read the words in each line. Write "S" on the line if the words have the same meaning. Write "D" on the line if the words have different meanings.

11.	give	take	_____
12.	little	tiny	_____
13.	high	low	_____
14.	ladies	women	_____
15.	push	hug	_____

What's Wrong Here?

Picture clues

Look carefully at the picture. Draw an "X" over objects that do not belong. Write the name of each object on the lines below. Then color the picture.

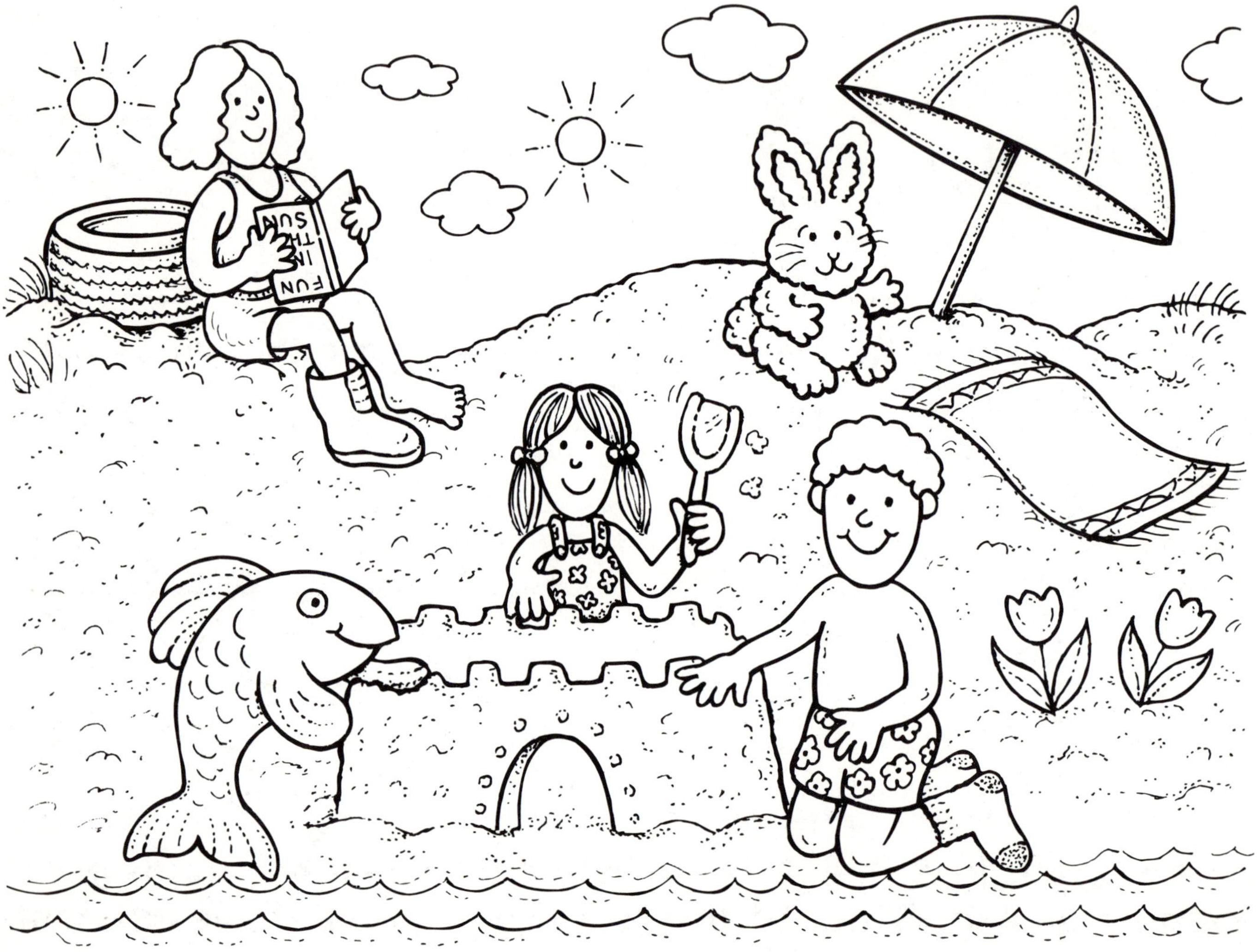

1. _____   5. _____

2. _____   6. _____

3. _____   7. _____

4. _____   8. _____

What Comes Next?

Week 2 — Patterns

Look at the shape pattern in each row. Then complete the pattern.

1. 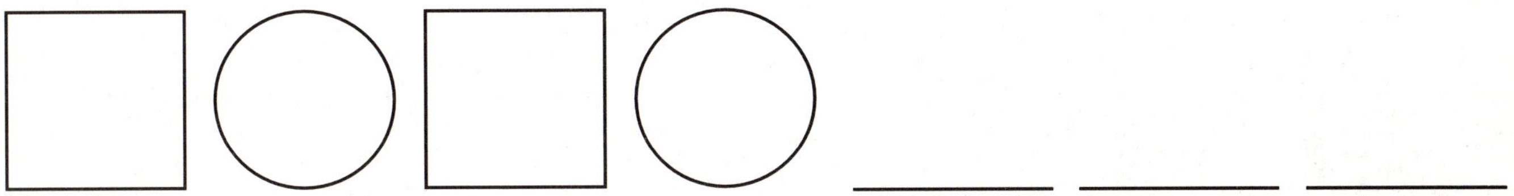 ☐ ◯ ☐ ◯ ___ ___ ___

2. 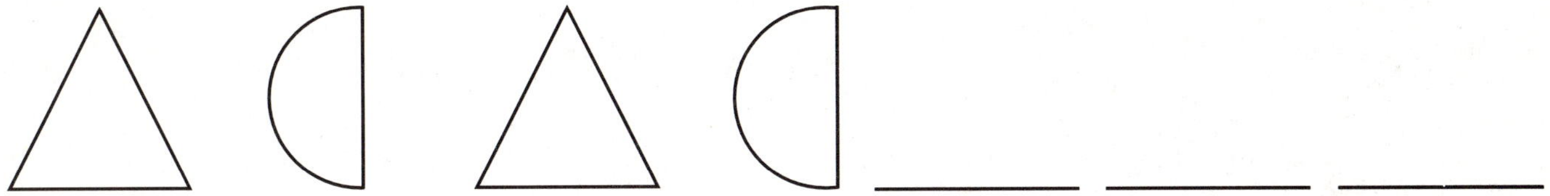 △ ◐ △ ◐ ___ ___ ___

3. 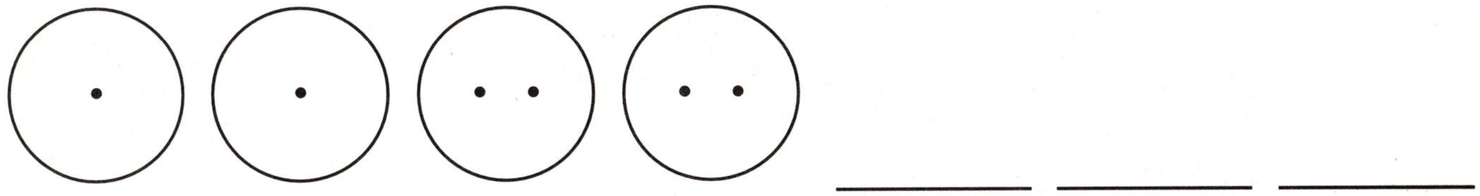 ◉(1) ◉(1) ◉(2) ◉(2) ___ ___ ___

4. 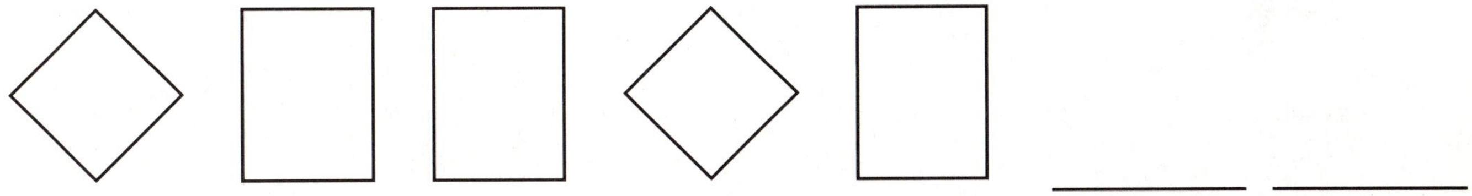 ◇ ▭ ▭ ◇ ▭ ___ ___ ___

5. 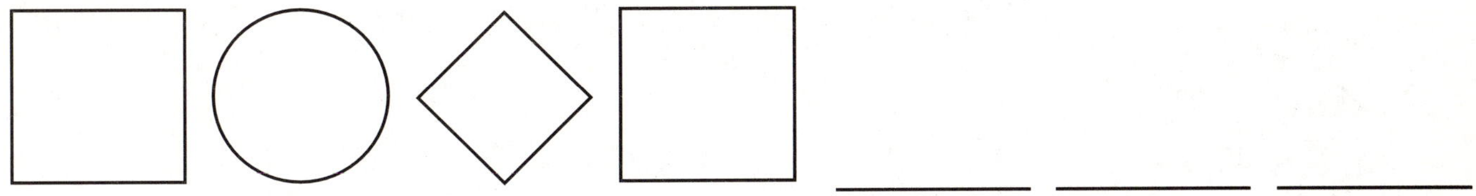 ☐ ◯ ◇ ☐ ___ ___ ___

6. 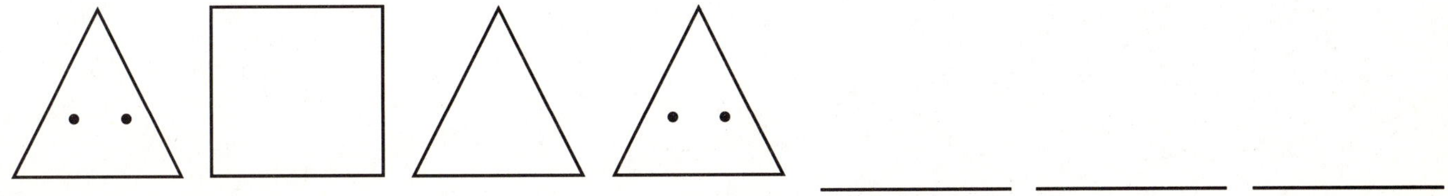 △(2) ☐ △ △(2) ___ ___ ___

Listen Carefully

Week 2
Phonics

Say the word for each picture. Listen to the last sound in each word. Then circle the words in each row that end with the same sound as the picture word.

1.	**doll**	deer	ball	pail	drink
2.	**ax**	apple	fox	ant	socks
3.	**cake**	car	fork	bike	train
4.	**drink**	drop	rink	rock	sink
5.	**house**	hose	mouse	desk	blouse
6.	**fish**	five	dish	splash	stove

Word Circus

Compound words

Read the compound words below. Then circle the two small words that make up each compound. Write the two small words on the lines. The first one is done for you.

1. (broom)(stick)   broom   stick
2. tablecloth _____ _____
3. sunshine   _____ _____
4. dishpan   _____ _____
5. classroom   _____ _____
6. bookcase   _____ _____
7. treetop   _____ _____
8. playground _____ _____
9. highway   _____ _____
10. suntan   _____ _____
11. campfire   _____ _____
12. birthday   _____ _____
13. bedroom   _____ _____
14. newspaper _____ _____

Word Magic

A long vowel sound is like the "i" in *kite*.
A short vowel sound is like the "i" in *grin*.
Read the words below. Write the words with a long vowel sound in the LONG column. Write the words with a short vowel sound in the SHORT column.

home	hit	might	wild	light
cut	take	last	place	bat
scrape	wash	pin	tub	black
bite	know	rub	felt	pipe

LONG **SHORT**

Fun with Fractions

Each object is divided into equal parts. Write a fraction that tells what part of each object is shaded.

Example:

1.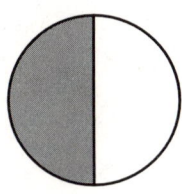

2.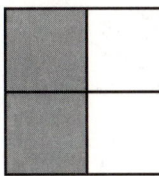

_____   _____

3.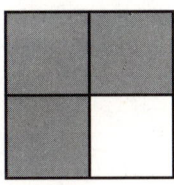

4.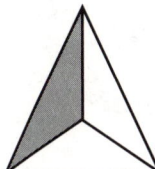

_____   _____

5.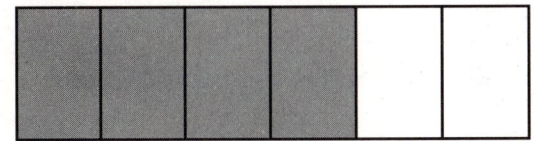

6.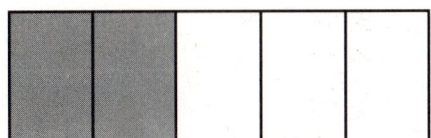

_____   _____

7.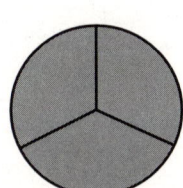

8.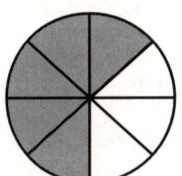

_____   _____

What Time Is It?

Telling time

Look at each clock. Then write the time shown on the line. The first one is done for you.

1. _____8:30_____   2. _____   3. _____

4. _____   5. _____   6. _____

7. _____   8. _____   9. _____

10. _____   11. _____   12. _____

Picture Clues

Drawing conclusions

Look carefully at each picture. Write who the person is in the picture. Then write clues from the picture that helped you figure it out. Finally, write a sentence describing what is happening in the picture.

1. Person:_____
   Clues: _____
   Description:_____

2. Person:_____
   Clues:_____
   Description:_____

Punctuation, Please!

Some sentences tell about something. These are statements. Other sentences ask something. These are questions. Rewrite these sentences so they end with a period or a question mark.

1. The bedroom in my new house is painted blue

   _____

2. Where do you go to school

   _____

3. Do you like to take the school bus

   _____

4. All my new friends are very nice

   _____

5. The teacher took our class on a trip

   _____

6. What is your favorite school subject

   _____

All Aboard!

Week 3

Addition, subtraction

Add or subtract to find the answers.

1. 6 + 0 =

2. 6 + 30 =

3. 6 + 6 =

4. 36 − 6 =

5. 12 + 6 =

6. 18 − 6 =

7. 18 + 6 =

8. 12 − 6 =

9. 24 + 6 =

10. 15 − 6 =

11. 6 − 6 =

12. 24 − 6 =

Daily Schedule

Week 3
Telling time

What does Will do each day? What time does he do it? Read Will's schedule. Then answer the questions below.

Will's Schedule
I get up at 7:30 a.m.
School starts at 8:30 a.m.
I come home from school at 3:30 p.m.
I go outside to play at 4:00 p.m.
I start my homework at 4:30 p.m.
I eat dinner at 6:00 p.m.
I play with my dog at 7:00 p.m.
I start to read at 7:30 p.m.
I go to sleep at 8:30 p.m.

1. What time does Will's school start?
   _____

2. What time does Will come home from school?
   _____

3. What time does Will go outside to play? How long can he play?
   _____

4. Does Will do his homework before or after dinner?
   _____

5. What does Will do after eating dinner?
   _____

6. How long does Will read before going to sleep?
   _____

One or More?

Week 3 — Plurals

Read each sentence. Then write the word that correctly completes the sentence on the line.

1. We bought six _____ to make a pie.
   (apple, apples)

2. The two _____ played in the park all day.
   (puppy, puppies)

3. Three large _____ ran down the street.
   (dog, dogs)

4. Our _____, Ms. Scott, took our class to the zoo.
   (teacher, teachers)

5. Sarah's birthday _____ is on Saturday.
   (party, parties)

6. My three _____ will play in the ball game this weekend.
   (friend, friends)

7. All the _____ enjoyed acting in the class play.
   (child, children)

8. Three _____ in my reading book are very funny.
   (story, stories)

9. Did you see Sam's _____, Rosie, run down the street?
   (cat, cats)

10. We found a gold _____ in the grass.
    (ring, rings)

Making One Into Two

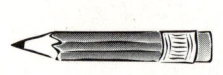

Week 3 — Contractions

The contraction in each sentence is underlined. Read the sentence. Then find the two words in the box that make up the contraction. Write the two words on the lines. The first one is done for you.

I will	He is
I am	Here is
You will	She will
He would	I would
We have	They will
There is	She would

1. <u>You'll</u> have to cut the cake.   You   will

2. <u>I'll</u> be in school tomorrow.

3. <u>She'd</u> like to be on our team.

4. <u>We've</u> studied hard for the test.

5. Now <u>I'm</u> going to read the story.

6. <u>There's</u> your dog in the park.

7. <u>He'd</u> like to go to the zoo with us.

8. <u>They'll</u> carry the boat to the lake.

9. <u>Here's</u> the book we need for school.

10. <u>She'll</u> ride a pony at the fair.

11. <u>He's</u> not swimming today.

12. <u>I'd</u> like to make dinner tonight.

Ounces or Pounds?

Ounces are used to measure the weight of very light objects. Pounds are used to measure the weight of heavy objects. Look at each picture. Then decide if you would use ounces or pounds to measure the weight of each object. Circle your answer.

1.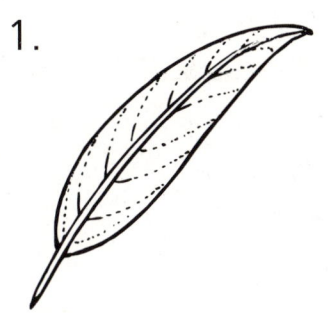
ounces   pounds

2.
ounces   pounds

3.
ounces   pounds

4.
ounces   pounds

5.
ounces   pounds

6.
ounces   pounds

7.
ounces   pounds

8.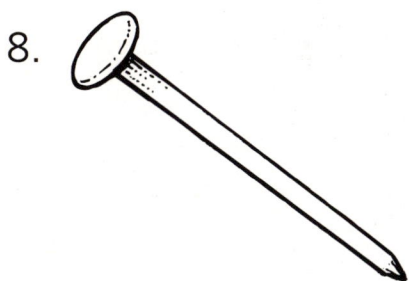
ounces   pounds

9.
ounces   pounds

Number Fair

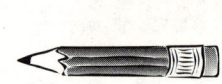

Week 3
Multiplication

Write each multiplication number sentence. Then multiply to find the answer. For example:

$$2 \times 2 = 4$$

1.  ____ x ____ = ____

2. 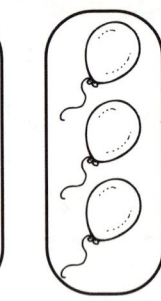 ____ x ____ = ____

3.  ____ x ____ = ____

4.  ____ x ____ = ____

5. 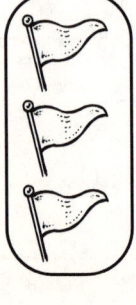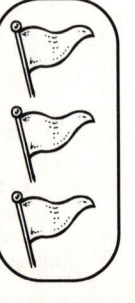 ____ x ____ = ____

Punctuation Party

Week 4
Punctuation, capitalization

Sentences that make a statement end with a period. Sentences that express strong feelings end with an exclamation point. Look at the examples below, then rewrite the sentences that follow with correct capitalization and punctuation.

my mother bought a new sweater	My mother bought a new sweater.
wow what a beautiful sweater	Wow, what a beautiful sweater!

1. we love to swim in the pool

   _____

2. the dog jumped in the pool

   _____

3. hurry up and jump in

   _____

4. lets eat hot dogs and chips

   _____

5. what a great day

   _____

6. i like marias bathing suit

   _____

7. everyone is going to eat lunch

   _____

8. jill doesn't like to swim

   _____

9. swim faster maria

   _____

10. this is so much fun

    _____

© Frank Schaffer Publications, Inc.   FS-23404 Summer Skills for the 2nd Grade Graduate

Word Hunt

Phonics — Week 4

Can you find the words that have the "sh" sound? Sometimes the "sh" sound is made by the letters "sh," as in *short*. Sometimes the "sh" sound is made by the letters "ti" as in *nation*. Say each word below. Circle the words with the "sh" sound.

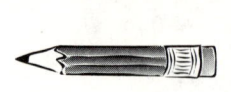

1.	sat	shut	so	vacation
2.	sometime	rush	attention	action
3.	shine	trash	tight	sight
4.	shoulder	shake	bake	sip
5.	show	bush	station	slip
6.	push	silk	relation	addition
7.	shun	crush	staff	subtraction
8.	laugh	clash	lotion	facts
9.	mention	stick	fresh	enough
10.	mash	notion	strife	tough

Order Up!

Week 1 — Alphabetizing

Read the words on each line. Underline the first letter of each word. Then write the words in alphabetical order on the lines.

A.   apple   return   everyone

1. _____   2. _____   3. _____

B.   horse   camp   food

1. _____   2. _____   3. _____

C.   special   mark   bee

1. _____   2. _____   3. _____

D.   like   week   piano

1. _____   2. _____   3. _____

E.   together   very   night

1. _____   2. _____   3. _____

F.   mom   pie   never

1. _____   2. _____   3. _____

A Piece of the Pie

 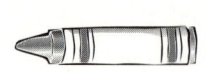 

Week 4 — Fractions

Each pie is divided into parts. Look at the fraction next to each pie. Then color the pie to show the fraction. The first one is done for you.

1. $\frac{1}{2}$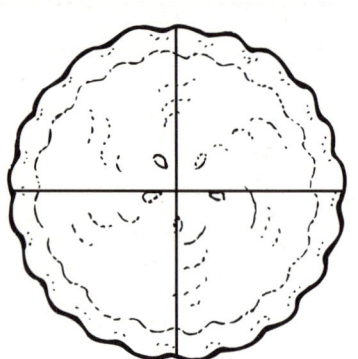

2. $\frac{1}{3}$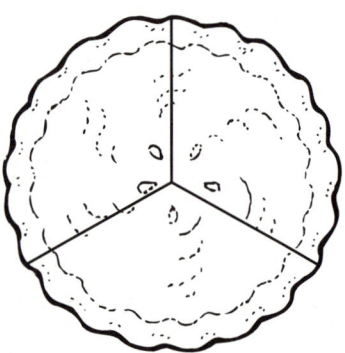

3. $\frac{3}{6}$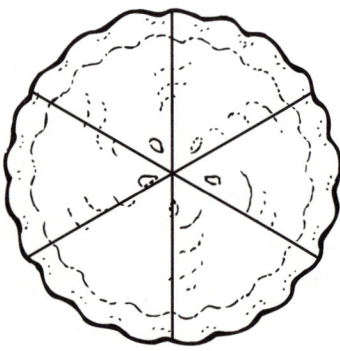

4. $\frac{4}{6}$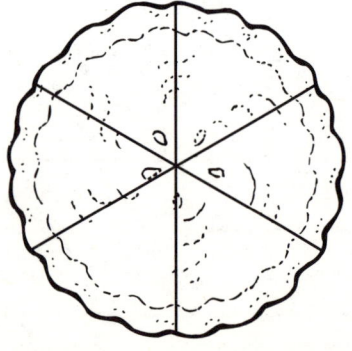

5. $\frac{3}{4}$

6. $\frac{2}{3}$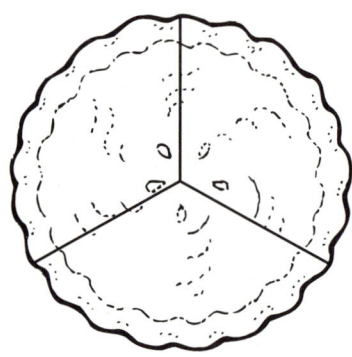

7. $\frac{1}{4}$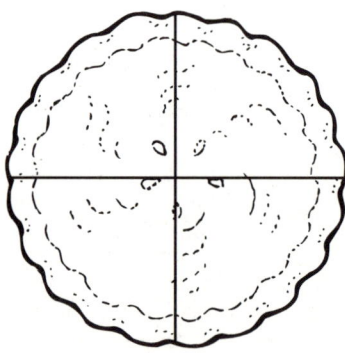

8. $\frac{5}{8}$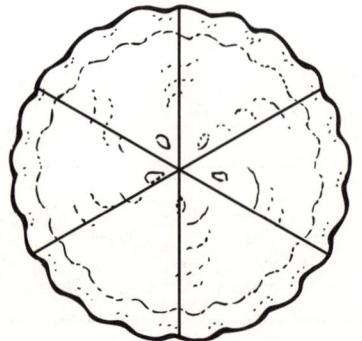

Story Puzzle

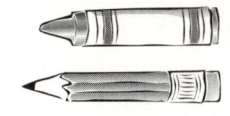 

Week 4
Sequencing

Look carefully at the pictures below. They tell a story. Then read the sentences. Each sentence tells about one picture. Put the sentences in order by writing the correct picture number on each line. Then color the pictures.

_____ José falls asleep after a busy day.
_____ José opens his birthday presents.
_____ José's parents get ready for his birthday party.
_____ José plays with his toys after the party.
_____ José wakes up on his birthday.
_____ José sees all his friends at his party.

1

2

3

4

5

6

© Frank Schaffer Publications, Inc.   FS-23404 Summer Skills for the 2nd Grade Graduate   41

Measure Up!

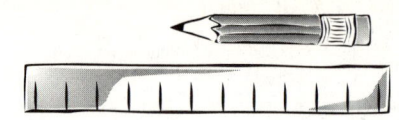 

Look at a ruler. There are 12 inches in one foot. Use your ruler to measure the following objects in your house.

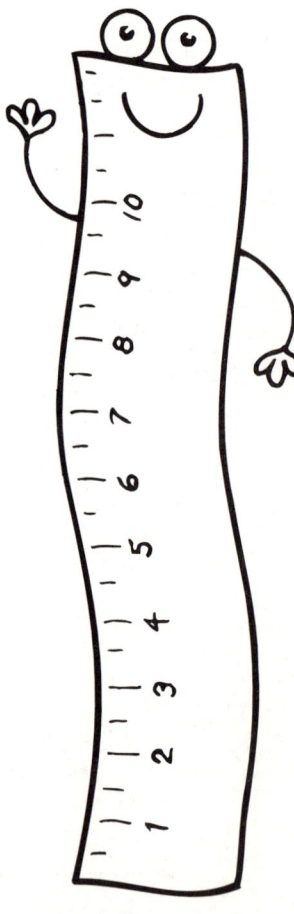

1. book _____ inches

2. fork _____ inches

3. pencil _____ inches

4. glass _____ inches

5. piece of paper _____ inches

6. eraser _____ inches

7. envelope _____ inches

8. small toy _____ inches

9. napkin _____ inches

10. noodle _____ inches

Number Patterns

Look at each group of numbers. Notice the pattern. Write the missing numbers on the lines.

1. 4   4   8   8   12   12   16   ___   20   ___

2. 20   18   ___   14   12   10   ___   6   ___

3. 3   6   9   ___   15   18   ___   24   ___

4. 25   25   20   20   15   ___   10   10   ___   ___

5. ___   21   ___   15   12   9   ___   ___   0

6. 2   4   6   8   ___   ___   ___   ___   ___

7. 5   10   15   20   ___   ___   ___   ___

8. 100   90   80   70   60   50   ___   ___   ___   ___

Hit a Home Run!

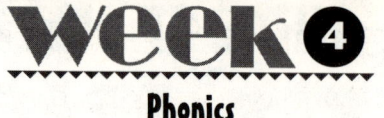

WEEK 4
Phonics

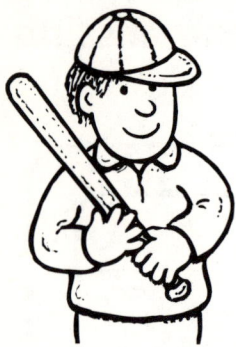

Some words begin with the soft "g" sound, as in *giraffe.* Other words start with the hard "g" sound, as in *gold.* Look at the words below. If the word begins with the soft "g" sound, write it in a soft "g" baseball diamond. If the word begins with the hard "g" sound, write it in a hard "g" baseball diamond.

gem	game	gold	geography
gift	gingerbread	give	globe
gentle	girl	gym	giant

Soft "g" Sound

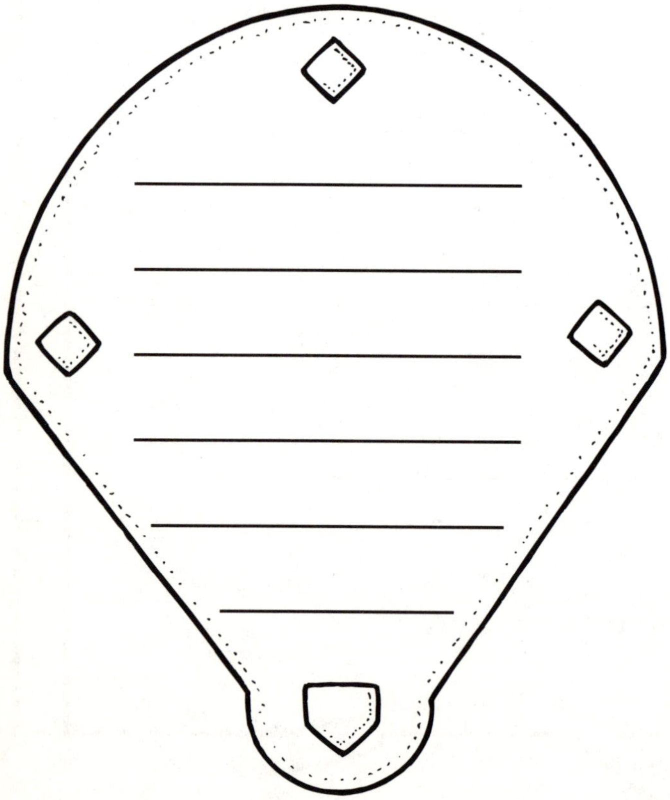

Hard "g" Sound

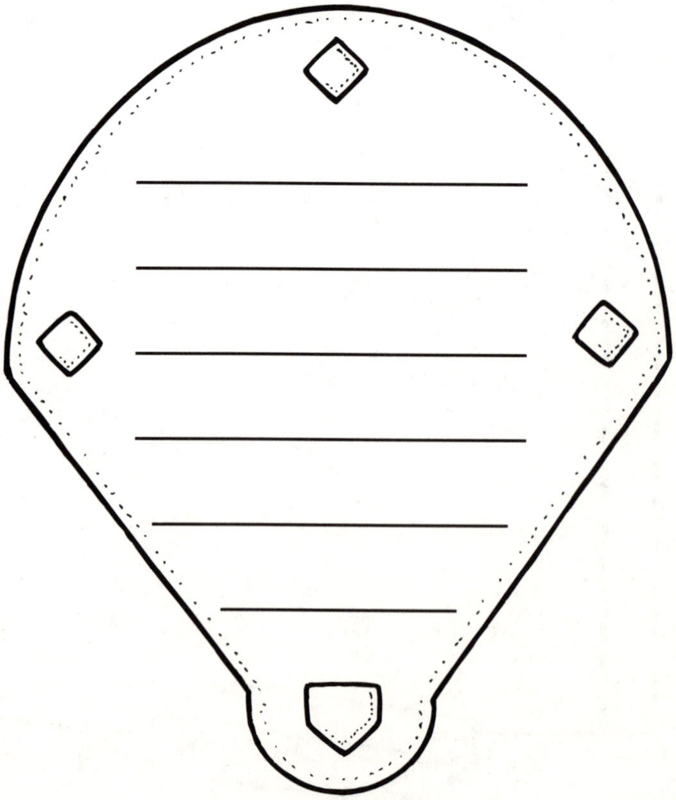

Count It Up!

Count the dollar bills and coins in each group. Write the amount of money on the line. Be sure to use a dollar sign and decimal point!

1. _____   (quarter, dime, nickel)

2. _____   (1 dollar bill, nickel)

3. _____   (1 dollar bill, 5 quarters)

4. _____   (1 dollar bill, quarter, dime)

5. _____   (2 dollar bills, dime, 2 nickels)

6. _____   (3 dollar bills, 2 quarters, nickel, dime)

7. _____   (3 quarters, dime, 2 nickels, 3 pennies)

On the Go

Word problems

Add or subtract to find the answers below. Show your work.

1. At the beginning of the trip, Ellen and Sam visited their grandmother's farm. There were 50 chickens, 22 horses, and 14 pigs on the farm. How many farm animals were there all together?

   Answer: _____

2. Their mother bought 90 gallons of gas in the first week of the trip. By the end of the week, they had 13 gallons left. How many gallons did they use?

   Answer: _____

3. Ellen wrote 10 postcards. Her brother Sam wrote 12. Her mother wrote 15. How many postcards did they write all together?

   Answer: _____

4. Ellen and Sam will travel 52 miles on Tuesday. They will travel 39 miles on Wednesday. How many miles will they travel all together?

   Answer: _____

5. The family visited a circus on Saturday. A clown was giving away balloons. In the morning, the clown had 80 balloons. He gave away 54 balloons. How many balloons did he have left at the end of the day?

   Answer: _____

Picture Clues

Context clues

Look at the picture below. Then circle the correct answer to each question based on the picture. Color the picture when you are finished.

1. Where is everyone playing?

   in the street　　　　　in the park　　　　　in school

2. What is Sam doing under the tree?

   playing ball　　　　　listening to a radio　　　　　reading

3. What is Juan feeding the squirrel?

   apples　　　　　peanuts　　　　　carrots

4. What kind of day is it?

   warm　　　　　cold　　　　　rainy

5. How does everyone feel?

   sad　　　　　scared　　　　　happy

6. What is Jenny throwing to Jason?

   football　　　　　frisbee　　　　　baseball

All Over Town

Categorizing

In Smithtown, USA, there are four places Anita likes to visit. She likes to go to the grocery store, the zoo, the clothing store, and school. Look at the words below. Write each word below the place in which each item might be found.

lion	apple	blouse	elephant	coat
milk	bear	tiger	student	hat
book	desk	teacher	chalk	monkey
shoe	gloves	tomato	beans	cake

Grocery Store

Zoo

Clothing Store

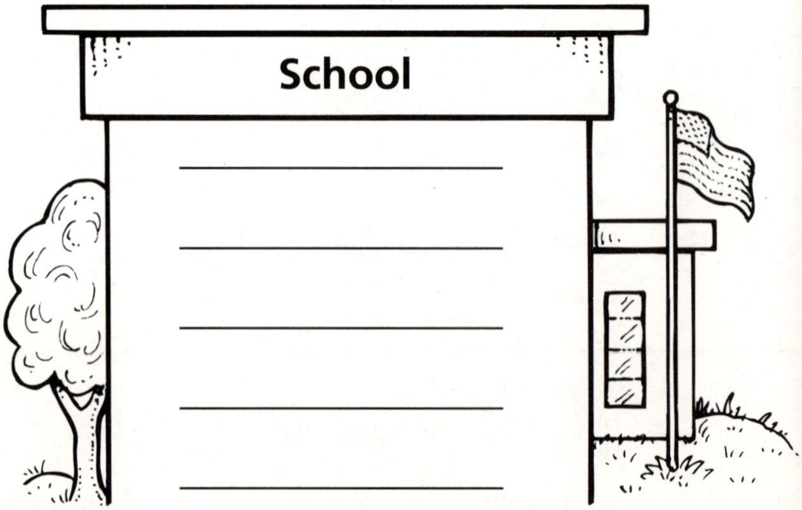

School

Syllable Stumper

Week 5
Syllables

Read each word. Circle the one-syllable words in red. Circle the two-syllable words in yellow. Circle the three-syllable words in green.

brave	table	
able	difficult	
little	hillside	
adult	adventure	but
friendly	looking	middle
head	easy	hard
telephone	important	computer
glass	tissue	book
after	microphone	picture
ball	desk	apple

Make Your Place

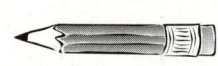

Week 5
Place value

Write each number in the correct column. Write the complete number on the line.

1. 5 in the tens place
   6 in the ones place   = | Tens | Ones |
   |---|---|
   | | | = _____

2. 7 in the tens place
   9 in the ones place   = | Tens | Ones |
   |---|---|
   | | | = _____

3. 1 in the hundreds place
   0 in the tens place
   9 in the ones place   = | Hundreds | Tens | Ones |
   |---|---|---|
   | | | | = _____

4. 9 in the hundreds place
   2 in the tens place
   7 in the ones place   = | Hundreds | Tens | Ones |
   |---|---|---|
   | | | | = _____

5. 6 in the hundreds place
   3 in the tens place
   8 in the ones place   = | Hundreds | Tens | Ones |
   |---|---|---|
   | | | | = _____

6. 2 in the thousands place
   0 in the hundreds place
   1 in the tens place
   8 in the ones place   = | Thousands | Hundreds | Tens | Ones |
   |---|---|---|---|
   | | | | | = _____

7. 4 in the thousands place
   4 in the hundreds place
   4 in the tens place
   6 in the ones place   = | Thousands | Hundreds | Tens | Ones |
   |---|---|---|---|
   | | | | | = _____

Rhyme Time

Week 5 — Rhyming words

Read the first word in each row. Then read the words that follow. Circle all the words that rhyme with the first word.

1.	**sick**	stick	pick	put	sit
2.	**sew**	son	mow	ripe	row
3.	**link**	drink	sink	rink	rang
4.	**trap**	wrap	clip	clap	tap
5.	**bike**	bat	like	let	Mike
6.	**pig**	dig	big	bag	did
7.	**bear**	chair	wear	care	say
8.	**just**	dirt	dust	row	rust
9.	**stop**	top	lit	mop	mitt
10.	**king**	sing	swing	wing	back

Plural Power

Plurals

Complete each sentence by writing the plural of the word in parenthesis on the line. Sometimes you will add an "s" to the word. However, if a word ends in "y," change the "y" to "i" and add "es." For example, *fly = flies.*

1. I have two pet _____. (cat)

2. There are two Halloween _____ this year. (party)

3. All the _____ ran across the field. (pony)

4. Maria loves all her new _____. (gift)

5. Did you eat the big bag of _____? (cherry)

6. Larry will visit two _____ on his trip. (country)

7. I will return the _____ to the library. (book)

8. The _____ fell off the table. (bowl)

9. I climbed three _____ on Sunday! (tree)

10. I want to hear both _____. (story)

All About Henry

Read the story. Then answer the questions below.

Henry the pig loved to play on the big farm. He lived there with his mother, father, and seven brothers and sisters. Henry's mother said to him, "Do not walk far from home. If you do, you will get lost."

Early one morning, Henry ate his breakfast with his sister, Emily. Then they played outside. Finally, Emily went inside the barn to take a nap.

Now Henry was all alone. He decided to take a walk. First he crossed the big field near the barn. Then he went to the lake. Finally, he fell asleep under a big apple tree. When Henry woke up, it was dark.

"Oh, my," cried Henry. "Where is my mother? Where is my father? Where is my sister? I want my dinner!" Then he started to cry.

1. Where did Henry live?

   _____

2. What is the first thing Henry did in the morning?

   _____

3. Where did Henry and Emily play?

   _____

4. After Emily left, what did Henry do first?

   _____

5. Where did Henry fall asleep?

   _____

On another sheet of paper, write what you think Henry will do next.

Spending Spree!

Week 6
Money

Look at the money in each row. Then look at the price of each object. If the money is enough to buy the object, write *yes* on the line. If the money is not enough to buy the object, write *no*.

1. _____   (toy car ¢.65) — 3 quarters

2. _____   (football $5.00) — 4 one-dollar bills, 3 quarters

3. _____   (doll $2.35) — 1 one-dollar bill, 5 quarters, 2 dimes

4. _____   (purse $1.99) — 6 quarters, 4 nickels

5. _____   (candy $1.19) — 3 quarters, 2 dimes, 2 pennies

6. _____   (book $3.50) — 2 one-dollar bills, 5 dimes, 3 nickels

Number Hunt

Addition, subtraction

Fill in the missing numbers to complete the number sentences.

1. 7 + ____ = 7
2. 8 + ____ = 16
3. 7 + ____ + 7 = 21
4. ____ + 10 = 24
5. 21 + ____ = 27
6. ____ − 7 = 0
7. ____ − 5 = 23
8. 35 − ____ = 26
9. 14 − ____ = 10
10. ____ − 8 = 13

11. ____ + 10 = 20
12. ____ + 5 = 30
13. ____ + 3 + 3 = 9
14. 10 − ____ = 4
15. 15 − ____ = 9
16. 25 − ____ = 15
17. ____ − 5 = 5
18. ____ − 7 = 5

Ride the Number Train

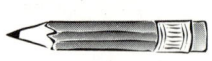

Week 6
Multiplication

Multiply to find each answer.

1. 6 train cars x 4 people in each car.

   How many people in all? _____

2. 3 train cars x 10 people in each car.

   How many people in all? _____

3. 5 train cars x 2 people in each car.

   How many people in all? _____

4. 3 train cars x 4 people in each car.

   How many people in all? _____

At the Zoo

Parts of speech

A *noun* is a person, place, or thing. Read each sentence carefully. Then circle the noun(s). The first one is done for you.

1. The (monkeys) play all day.

2. The trees are tall and green.

3. The sun is very hot.

4. Mother is looking around.

5. My friend came too.

6. The zoo is fun.

7. Koalas are cute.

8. The tigers roar.

9. Giraffes have long necks.

10. The bears growl.

11. Zebras can run very fast.

12. The elephants like to eat peanuts.

13. Snakes aren't slimy at all!

14. My favorite animal is the lion.

15. The kangaroos are funny.

16. Why do hyenas laugh at us?

17. We feed the seals fish.

18. Penguins are birds that can't fly.

Up to 100

Numerical order

Fill in the missing numbers in the chart.

1	2	3		5	6		8	9	10
			14			17			20
21	22			25	26			29	
		33				37			
41			44		46		48		50
	52			55				59	
		63				67			70
71			74				78		
	82				86				90
		93		95			98		

On the Playground

Parts of speech

An *adjective* describes a noun. Read each sentence. Then circle the adjective that describes each noun. Hint: There may be more than one noun and adjective.

1. The happy children are playing.

2. Several children squealed as they slid down the yellow slide.

3. The nice teacher watched as the noisy children played.

4. Maria and Sam made a big house with new blocks.

5. Children stood in a long line for the red swingset.

6. Juan and Tessa jumped rope on the cool, green grass.

7. The sandbox was filled with laughing children.

8. The warm sun feels good.

9. The little babies cried a lot.

10. We played many fun games.

Fun in the Sun

Parts of speech

Read each sentence. The subject is in bold. Circle the verb that tells what the subject is doing.

1. **The children** play happily in the sand.

2. **The warm wind** blows the waves onto the shore.

3. **Anna** builds a sandcastle with her sister.

4. **Her brother** knocks the sandcastle over!

5. **The sun** feels hot on their backs.

6. **Josh** is collecting shells.

7. **Stacy** found a starfish!

8. **Waves** splash onto Marissa's feet.

9. **The dog** runs happily in the surf.

10. **Jesse's ice-cream cone** is melting!

Before or After?

Sequencing

Read each story. Then answer the questions by writing B for *before* or A for *after* on the lines.

Sam washed his dog Rosie today. First he bought special soap at the pet store. Then he put Rosie in the bathtub. He turned on the water and washed Rosie. After the bath, Sam dried Rosie with a big towel. Finally, he cleaned the bathroom. Now Rosie is clean and happy.

1. Did Sam clean the bathroom before or after he washed Rosie? _____

2. Did Sam buy special soap before or after he put Rosie in the bathtub? _____

3. Did Sam dry Rosie before or after he turned on the water? _____

Tina's class visited the Space Museum. The teacher bought tickets. Then she gave each child a map of the museum. Next, the class visited a room with pictures of spaceships. Afterwards, the children learned more about space travel. Then they ate lunch. When they returned to school, each child wrote a story about the museum.

4. Did the teacher buy tickets before or after she gave out maps? _____

5. Did the class eat lunch before or after they learned about space travel? _____

6. Did the children write a story before or after they visited the Space Museum? _____

In the Bucket

Phonics

Some words begin with a soft "c" sound, as in *circle*.
Some words begin with a hard "c" sound, as in *car*.
Look at the words below. Say each word and decide whether it has the hard "c" sound or the soft "c" sound. Then write the word in the correct bucket.

cent	curtain	city	come
cone	certain	comb	cymbal
cook	citizen	call	celery
color	camp	circus	cinder

Hard "c" Sound   **Soft "c" Sound**

I Need Some Order

Alphabetizing — Week 7

In what order would you file these words? Read each word. Then write the words in alphabetical order. Remember, if you have two words that start with the same letter, look at the second letter.

clap
cent
apple
down
goat
ant
tent
dirt
where
were
take
deer

A Higher Order

Fill in the missing numbers in the chart.

101	102	103			106	107			110
111	112		114	115			118	119	120
		123		125		127		129	
131			134		136		138		140
	142	143		145				149	
151			154		156	157			160
	162				166		168	169	
		173		175		177			180
181	182				186		188	189	
		193		195		197			200

A Day at the Fair

Word problems

Read each word problem carefully. Then add or subtract to find the answer. Show your work.

1. A clown gave away 50 balloons on Tuesday. He gave away 25 balloons on Wednesday. How many balloons did he give away all together?

   Answer: _____

2. Ellen and David are playing a game. They have to throw a ball into a net. Ellen scores 52 points. David scores 37 points. How many points did Ellen and David score together?

   Answer: _____

3. Javier and Tim bought toys at the fair. Javier paid $1.75 for a toy car. Tim paid $1.10 for a ball. How much money did they spend all together?

   Answer: _____

4. On Monday morning there were 85 tickets available for the fair. Then the ticket agent sold 34 of them. How many tickets are left?

   Answer: _____

5. Joan brought $4.50 to the fair. She spent $1.25. How much money does she have left?

   Answer: _____

Play Time!

Draw a line between the matching times. The first one is done for you.

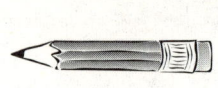

1. eleven o'clock in the morning — 4:30 p.m.

2. six o'clock in the evening — 4:00 a.m.

3. four-thirty in the afternoon — 11:00 a.m.

4. four o'clock in the morning — 7:30 p.m.

5. eight o'clock in the morning — 10:30 a.m.

6. six-thirty in the morning — 9:00 p.m.

7. seven-thirty in the evening — 6:00 p.m.

8. nine o'clock at night — 8:00 a.m.

9. ten-thirty in the morning — 6:30 a.m.

10. ten o'clock at night — 10:00 p.m.

Solve a Riddle

Blends

Read each question. Then complete the answer by writing the correct letter blend.

1. What flies from city to city? (gr pl sl) _____ ane

2. What rides on a railroad track? (tr cl cr) _____ ain

3. Who is someone you play with? (br tw fr) _____ iend

4. Where does a bird build a nest? (tw tr sl) _____ ee

5. What grows in a garden? (fl gl gr) _____ ower

6. What do people do in a car? (gl pr dr) _____ ive

7. What gets you high on a playground? (sc tr sw) _____ ing

8. What do you do after watching a show? (cl tr fr) _____ ap

9. What do you see on a busy road? (tr bl gl) _____ affic

10. What do you put your food on? (sc pl gl) _____ ate

© Frank Schaffer Publications, Inc.   FS-23404 Summer Skills for the 2nd Grade Graduate

Man's Best Friend

Odd & even numbers

Follow the Color Key to color the picture below.

Color Key
Odd numbers under 50 = red   Even numbers between 50 and 100 = green
Even numbers under 50 = blue Odd numbers between 50 and 100 = black
Even numbers over 100 = brown

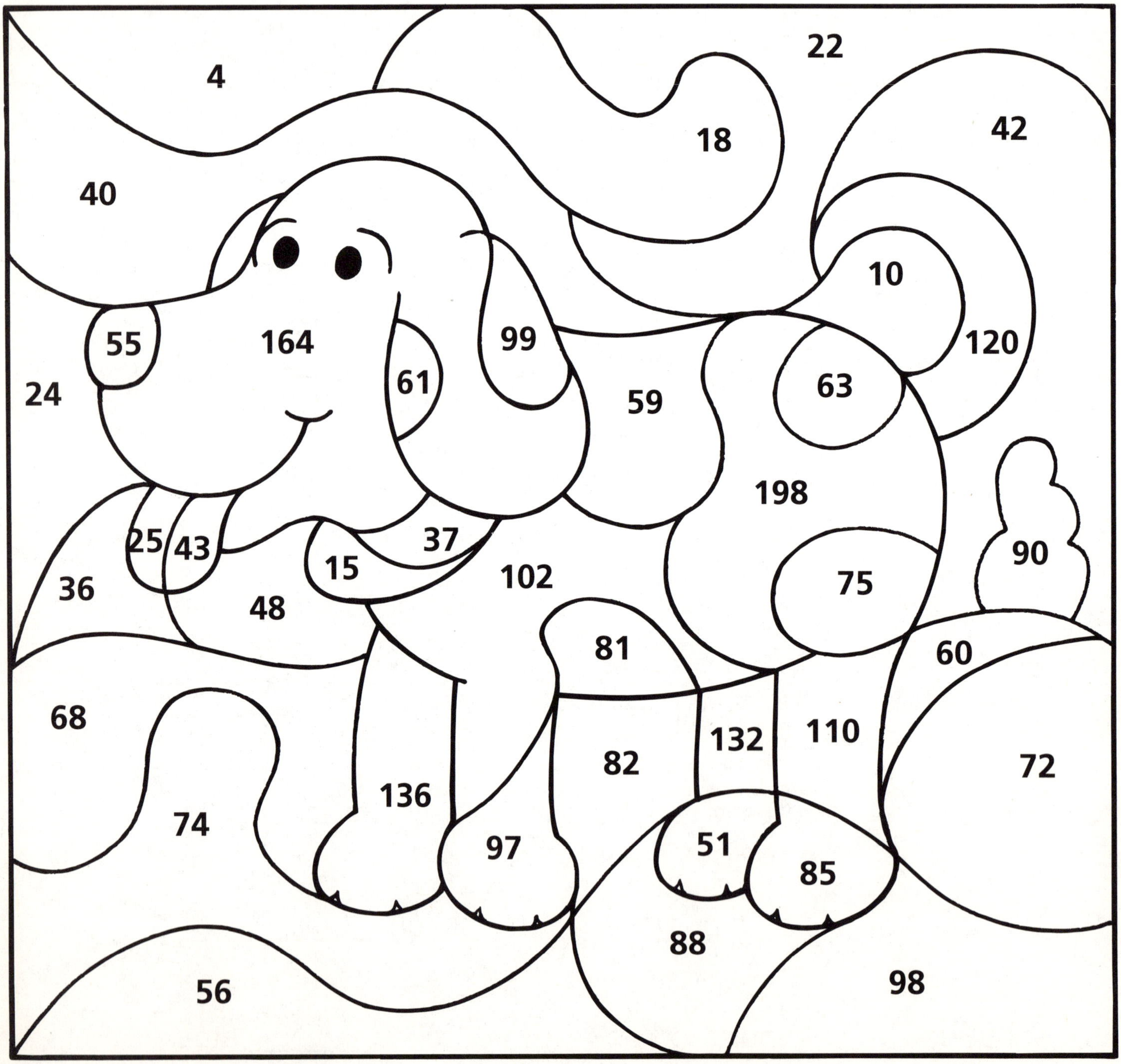

Sunny Syllables

Read the words in the box. Write two-syllable words in the suns. Write three-syllable words in the shells. Then draw lines dividing the words into syllables.

doctor	history	homemade	relative	corner
calculate	teacher	timetable	pencil	beautiful
permission	playground	afternoon	buying	decorate
basketball	action	address	justify	camel

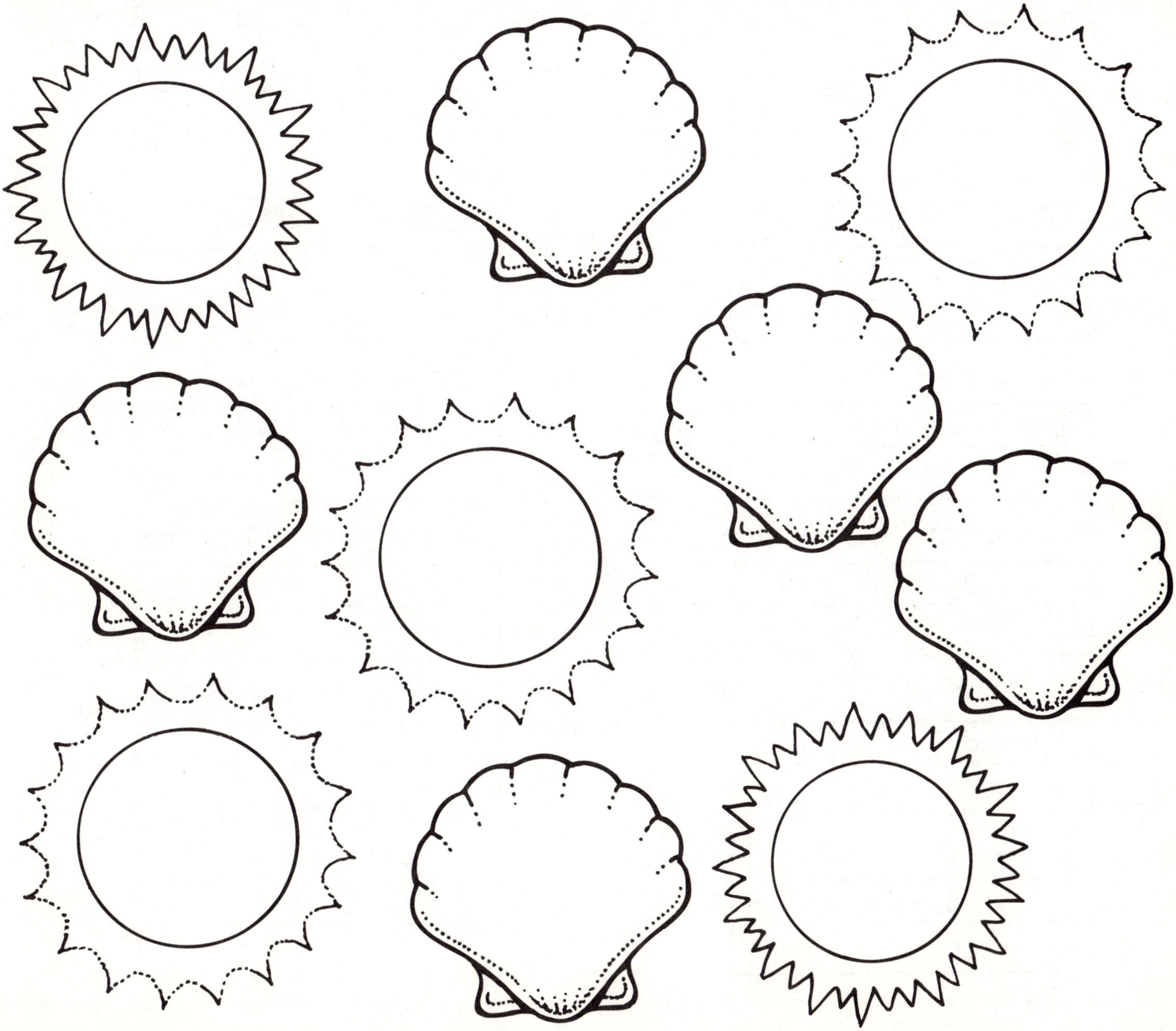

The Right Place

Place value

Write each number inside the correct box (hundreds, tens, or ones).

1. One hundred forty-six

Hundreds	Tens	Ones

2. Four hundred eighty

Hundreds	Tens	Ones

3. Six hundred ninety-seven

Hundreds	Tens	Ones

4. Nine hundred eighteen

Hundreds	Tens	Ones

5. Seven hundred twenty-five

Hundreds	Tens	Ones

6. Two hundred fifty-five

Hundreds	Tens	Ones

7. Three hundred thirty

Hundreds	Tens	Ones

8. One hundred eleven

Hundreds	Tens	Ones

9. Five hundred three

Hundreds	Tens	Ones

10. Eight hundred nine

Hundreds	Tens	Ones

11. Two hundred thirty-seven

Hundreds	Tens	Ones

12. One hundred eighty-nine

Hundreds	Tens	Ones

13. Three hundred seventy-one

Hundreds	Tens	Ones

14. Five hundred twenty-three

Hundreds	Tens	Ones

15. Nine hundred seventy-five

Hundreds	Tens	Ones

16. One hundred thirty-three

Hundreds	Tens	Ones

Pirate's Treasure

Capitalization

Some words always begin with a capital letter, such as names of people, states, days of the week, and holidays. Read the words in the treasure chest. Then write each word in the appropriate column. Be sure to capitalize the correct words!

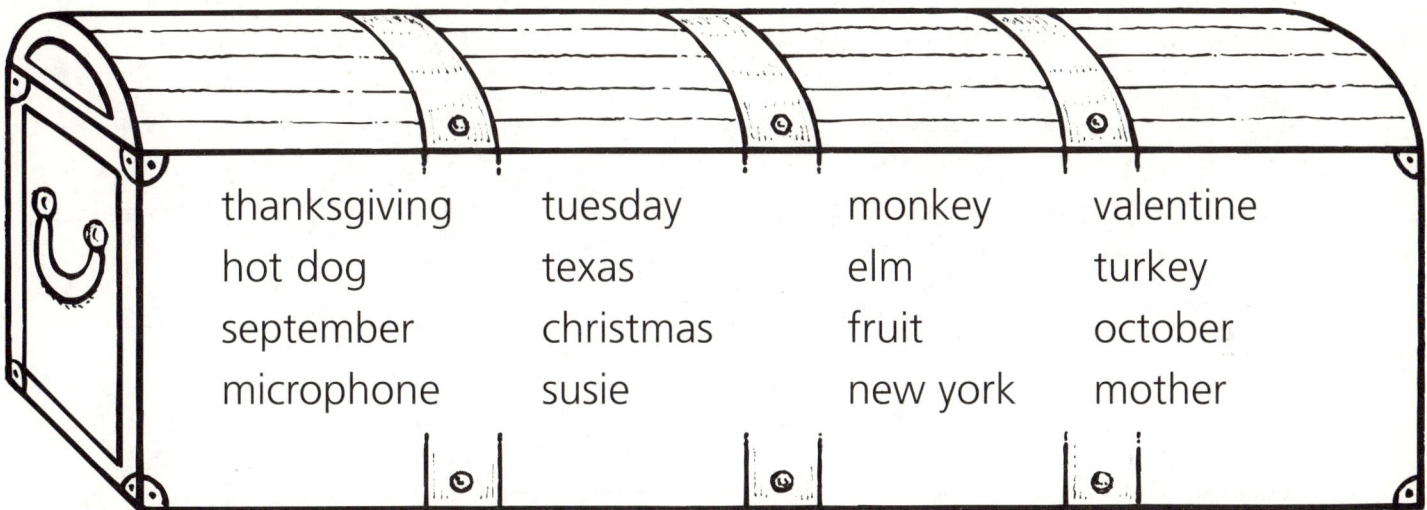

thanksgiving   tuesday   monkey   valentine
hot dog   texas   elm   turkey
september   christmas fruit   october
microphone   susie   new york   mother

Capitalized   **Not Capitalized**

Number Garden

Subtraction

Subtract to find the answers. Remember to regroup. When you are finished, color the flowers according to the Color Key.

Color Key	
between 9 and 20 = yellow	between 41 and 50 = purple
between 21 and 30 = blue	between 51 and 60 = green
between 31 and 40 = red	between 60 and 70 = orange

A. 37 − 28   63 − 47   52 − 28   44 − 18

B. 95 − 28   93 − 37   81 − 19   30 − 14

C. 91 − 45   56 − 17   90 − 58   50 − 12

D. 82 − 33   98 − 39   56 − 17   91 − 45

At the Art Fair

Read what happened to Maria and Thomas at the school art fair. Then answer the questions.

Today is a big day for Maria and Thomas. It's the school art fair. They are helping at the third-grade booth. Everyone in their class worked hard on their art projects. Maria painted two beautiful pictures. Thomas made a sailboat out of wood. Their friend, Anna, made a necklace from seashells. Late in the afternoon, Maria and Thomas will visit the other booths at the fair. They can't wait to see what else is for sale.

1. Why is this a big day for Maria and Thomas?

   _____

2. What are Maria and Thomas doing at the fair?

   _____

3. What did Thomas make?

   _____

4. What did Anna make?

   _____

5. What will Maria and Thomas do later in the day?

   _____

What else do you think Maria and Thomas might see at the art fair? On another sheet of paper, write about the rest of Maria's and Thomas's day at the art fair.

Time Out

Telling time

Look carefully at each clock. Then write the exact time on the line.

1. _____8:05_____   2. _____   3. _____

4. _____   5. _____   6. _____

7. _____   8. _____   9. _____

Story Stumpers

Word problems

Add or subtract to find the answer to each word problem. Show your work.

1. On Monday morning, 91 visitors came to the library. By noon, 47 of the visitors had left. How many visitors were still at the library?

   Answer: _____

2. There were 86 books returned to the library on Tuesday. By Wednesday, 47 of these books were borrowed by other people. How many books were left?

   Answer: _____

3. On Wednesday, 38 children visited the library. On Thursday, 26 children visited the library. How many children visited the library all together?

   Answer: _____

4. Many people give books to the library. In July, people gave 96 books to the library. In August, people gave 48 books to the library. How many books were given to the library all together?

   Answer: _____

5. The library isn't open every day during the summer. In June, the library was open 30 days. In August, the library was open 18 days. How many more days was it open in June than in August?

   Answer: _____

© Frank Schaffer Publications, Inc.   FS-23404 Summer Skills for the 2nd Grade Graduate

Past or Present?

Verb tense

Present-tense verbs tell about something that is happening now. Past-tense verbs tell about something that has already happened. Read each sentence. Write the verb on the line. Then write *present* or *past* to show the verb tense. The first one is done for you.

1. Our class worked hard on the play.
   _____worked_____ _____past_____

2. Our teacher, Ms. Morgan, helped us.
   _____ _____

3. Sam and Jessica planned our costumes.
   _____ _____

4. All the children study quietly.
   _____ _____

5. First, Mark talks about the play.
   _____ _____

6. Then, he answers any questions.
   _____ _____

7. Everyone sat quietly at the beginning of the play.
   _____ _____

8. All the students laughed at the funny song.
   _____ _____

9. The play receives a standing ovation.
   _____ _____

10. The students want to perform another play next year.
    _____ _____

Common or Proper?

Parts of speech, capitalization

A *common noun* is a person, place, or thing. A *proper noun* is the name of a person, place, or thing. Write each common and proper noun in the correct column. Capitalize words when needed.

oak avenue	anna	vegetable	new york
ocean	blouse	smith bakery	uncle joe
frank jones	birthday	street	tuesday
friend	december	girl	sister

Common Nouns **Proper Nouns**

Play Ball!

Graphing

Read the graph. It gives facts about the number of games won by baseball teams at Elm Street School. Then answer the questions.

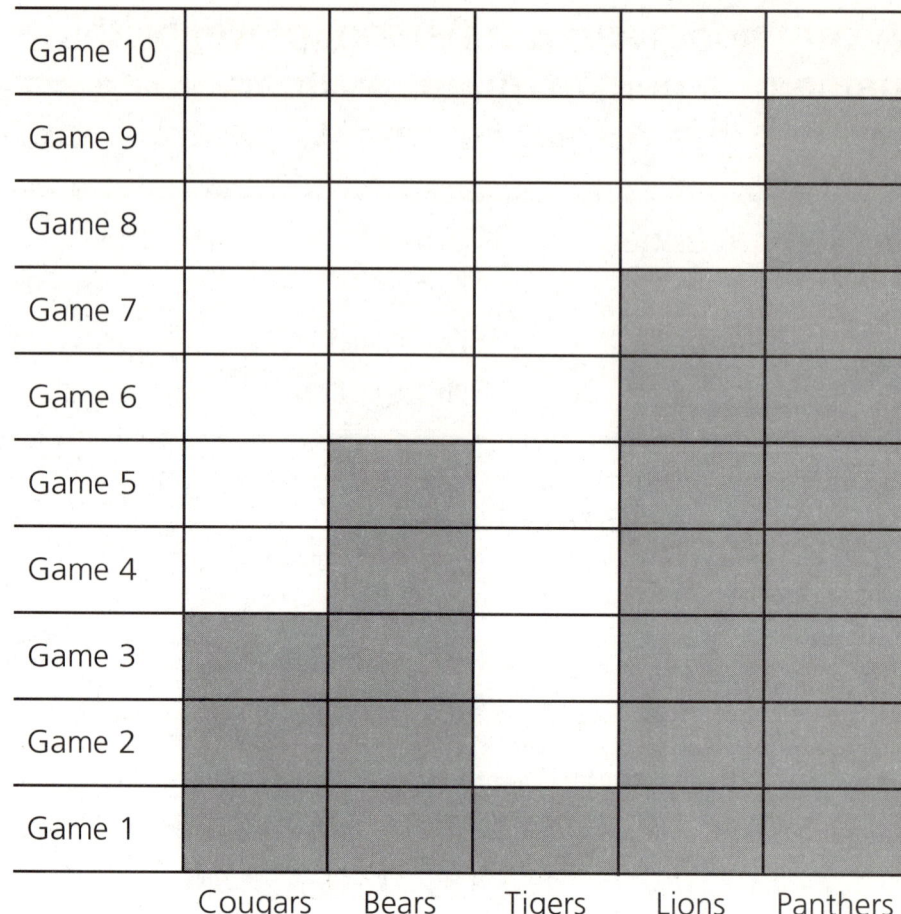

1. How many baseball games did the Cougars win? _____

2. How many baseball games did the Lions win? _____

3. Which team won the most games? _____

4. Which team won the least games? _____

5. Did the Bears win more or less games than the Cougars? _____

6. How many games did each team play? _____

Write It Right

Punctuation, capitalization

Read each sentence. Then rewrite the sentence, adding the correct puncutation and capitalization. The first one is done for you.

1. i was born on july 7 1990

   I was born on July 7, 1990.

2. will we leave for our vacation on august 3 1997

3. my older brother was twelve on april 11 1997

4. josés tenth birthday is on february 2 1998

5. someday I would love to visit washington d.c.

6. my best friend is from new york new york

7. did mr. morgan travel to portland oregon last summer

8. can we visit an art museum in los angeles california

Fishing for Numbers

Week 9 — Addition

Add to find the answer to each problem. Remember to regroup. When you are finished, color the fish according to the Color Key.

Color Key

between 9 and 20 = red	between 21 and 30 = green
between 31 and 40 = blue	between 41 and 50 = orange
between 51 and 60 = purple	between 61 and 70 = pink
between 71 and 80 = yellow	between 81 and 90 = brown

A. 38 + 12   11 + 7   45 + 26   37 + 27

B. 17 + 66   27 + 49   31 + 29   10 + 9

C. 16 + 26   26 + 26   18 + 8   12 + 19

D. 46 + 18   14 + 9   37 + 45   19 + 19

It's Mine

Apostrophes

An apostrophe is added to a word to show possession. For example: *Susan's cat is lost.* Read the sentences below. Rewrite the sentences adding an apostrophe where needed.

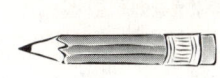

1. Mollys coat is in her room.

   _____

2. The dogs new toy is fun to play with.

   _____

3. Mr. Greens bookstore will open this Saturday.

   _____

4. I wore my mothers sweater at last nights concert.

   _____

5. The boys baseball broke Mrs. Henrys window.

   _____

6. The swimmers fins got lost in the oceans waves.

   _____

7. Where did Marias mother put the dogs leash?

   _____

Parachutes Away!

Place value

Count the hundreds, tens, and ones in each number. Then write out each number. The first one is done for you.

1.  461

   four hundreds

   six tens

   one one

2.  165

   _____

   _____

   _____

3.  294

   _____

   _____

   _____

4.  316

   _____

   _____

   _____

5.  964

   _____

   _____

   _____

6.  612

   _____

   _____

   _____

7. 537

   _____

   _____

   _____

8.  820

   _____

   _____

   _____

Pumpkin Patch

Some words in the pumpkins have a silent "e." Some do not. Color the pumpkins containing words with a silent "e."

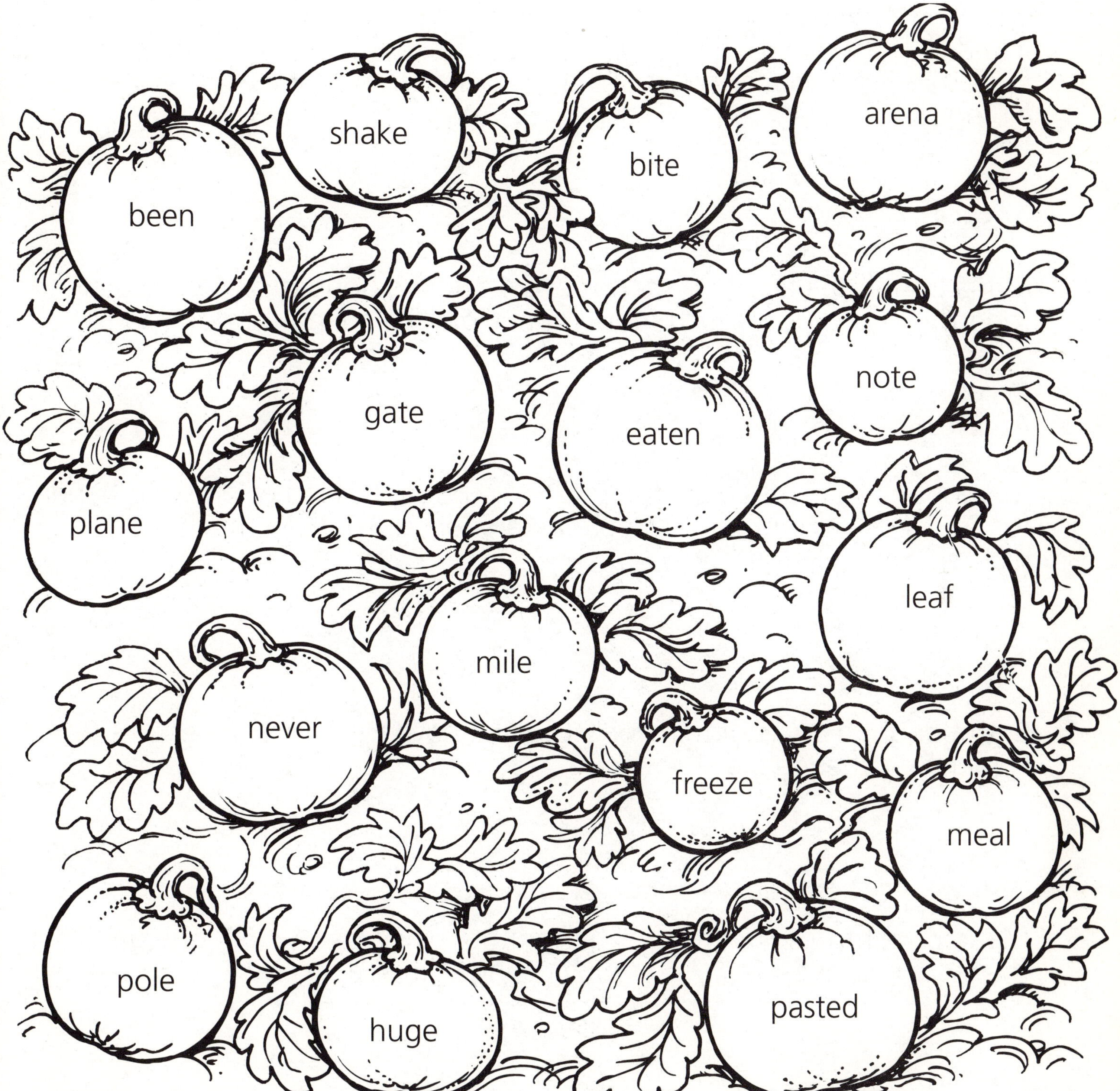

- shake
- bite
- arena
- been
- gate
- eaten
- note
- plane
- leaf
- never
- mile
- freeze
- meal
- pole
- huge
- pasted

To Market, to Market

Add or subtract to find the answer to each word problem. Show your work.

1. Lynn and Amy went to the store. Lynn bought a loaf of bread for $1.80. Amy bought pasta for $2.25. How much money did they spend all together?

    Answer: _____

2. Maria bought a bag of dog food for $4.28. She bought six cans of cat food for $2.35. How much more money did she spend for dog food?

    Answer: _____

3. Joe bought a box of paints for $1.26. He bought a pad of drawing paper for $2.08. He also bought some markers for $1.10. How much money did he spend all together?

    Answer: _____

4. Beth bought a quart of milk for $.85. She gave the store owner $1.00. How much change did she receive?

    Answer: _____

5. Maria bought fresh flowers for her mother. They cost $3.61. She gave the store owner $4.00. How much change did she receive?

    Answer: _____

More or Less?

Week 10 — Greater than/less than

Circle the greater number in each pair.

1) 29   31
2) 12   19
3) 55   35
4) 97   79
5) 42   45
6) 56   41
7) 67   76

8) 60   59
9) 20   30
10) 32   40

Circle the smaller number in each pair.

1) 7   9
2) 28   31
3) 90   80
4) 18   28
5) 45   44
6) 75   73
7) 99   98

8) 12   21
9) 41   39
10) 78 79
11) 25 52
12) 51 50
13) 22 29
14) 94 89

Picture This!

 **Week** 10
Homonyms

Some words sound alike but they have different spellings. They have different meanings, too. Look at each picture. Then circle the word that matches the picture.

1. eight   ate

2. rose   rows

3. bare   bear

4. would   wood

5. sun   son

6. flower   flour

7. dear   deer

Squirrel Feast

Addition, subtraction

Add or subtract to find the answers. Then color the acorns with answers over 100 to show Sydney Squirrel how to get home.

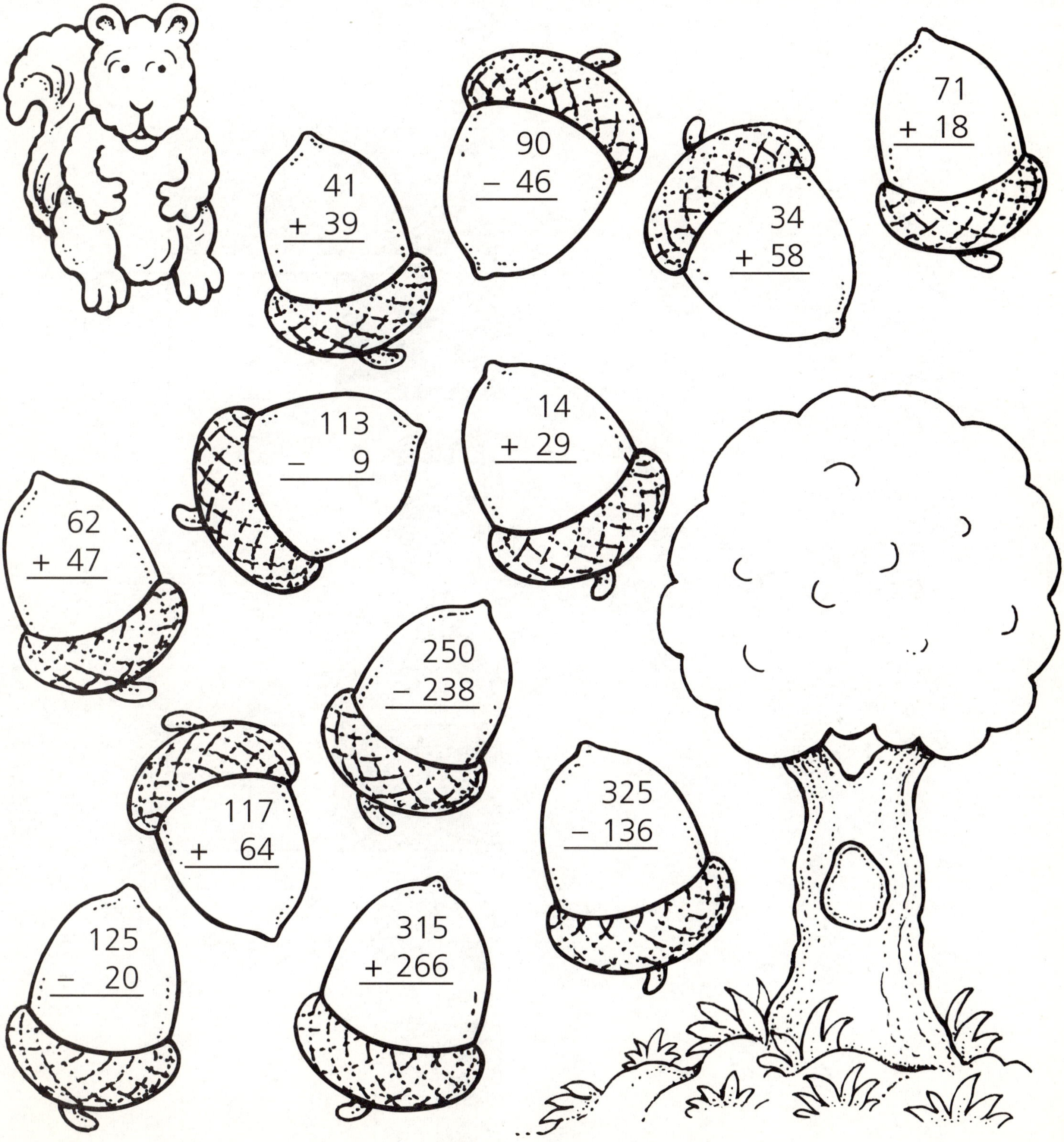

- 41 + 39
- 90 − 46
- 34 + 58
- 71 + 18
- 113 − 9
- 14 + 29
- 62 + 47
- 250 − 238
- 117 + 64
- 325 − 136
- 125 − 20
- 315 + 266

Match Up!

Draw a line matching each fraction to the correct picture.

1. $\frac{3}{4}$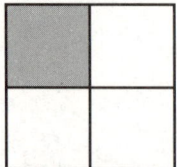

2. $\frac{1}{2}$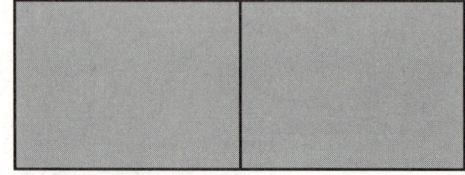

3. $\frac{2}{3}$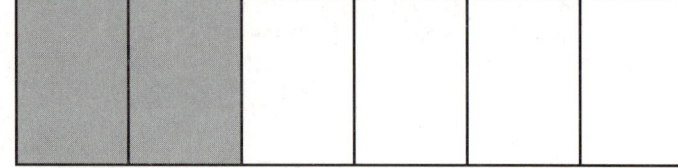

4. $\frac{5}{6}$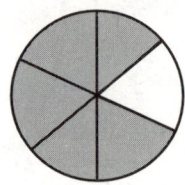

5. $\frac{2}{2}$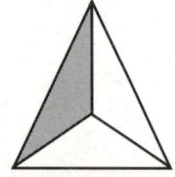

6. $\frac{1}{4}$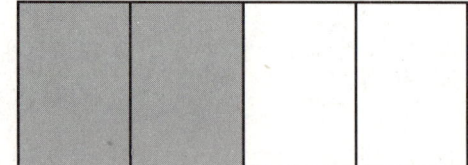

7. $\frac{1}{3}$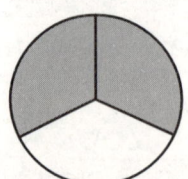

8. $\frac{2}{6}$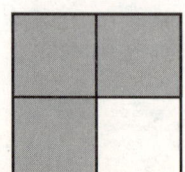

Hello, My Friend

Week 10
Letter writing

Write a letter to a friend telling him or her about your summer. Then color your stationery in bright summer colors.

_____
(Date)

Dear_____,

_____

_____

_____

_____

_____

_____

_____

Sincerely,

_____

Challenge a Friend!

Write your own word problems by filling in the numbers. Challenge a friend to try and solve the problems.

1. On Monday, Sam read _____ books. On Tuesday, Sam read _____ books. On Wednesday, he read _____ books. How many books did Sam read all together?

   Answer: _____

2. Ben hit _____ home runs when his team played the Cougars. Ben hit _____ home runs when his team played the Lions. Ben hit an amazing _____ home runs when his team played the Bears. How many home runs did Ben hit in all?

   Answer: _____

3. Juanita started out with _____ boxes of cookies to sell. She sold _____ boxes to her family. She sold _____ boxes to her friends. How many boxes does she have left?

   Answer: _____

4. Moesha had _____ dollars saved in her piggy bank. She decided to buy a small doll for _____. How much money does Moesha have left?

   Answer: _____

You're the Author!

week 10
Story writing

Look at the picture. Use your imagination to write a story about it, and then color it.

Greater or Smaller?

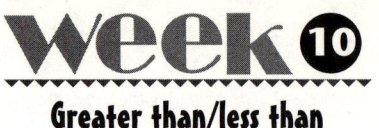

Compare the numbers below. Then write in the correct symbol.

< Less Than
> Greater Than

1. 21 _____ 19
2. 67 _____ 77
3. 37 _____ 42
4. 89 _____ 98
5. 98 _____ 89
6. 12 _____ 10
7. 15 _____ 50
8. 83 _____ 46
9. 45 _____ 55
10. 37 _____ 47
11. 88 _____ 18
12. 10 _____ 90
13. 77 _____ 17
14. 100 _____ 10
15. 33 _____ 31
16. 55 _____ 15
17. 80 _____ 70
18. 85 _____ 65

Congratulations!

_____

has put in that extra effort to be a star student!
Now you are ready for third grade!

Answer Key

Page 13
1. can, cat, cot
2. pear, pin, pet
3. bring, broil, bridge
4. star, stair, stage
5. mug, mat, mitt

Page 14
1. tiger
2. front
3. book
4. swing
5. jacket
6. swim
7. school
8. purple

Page 15

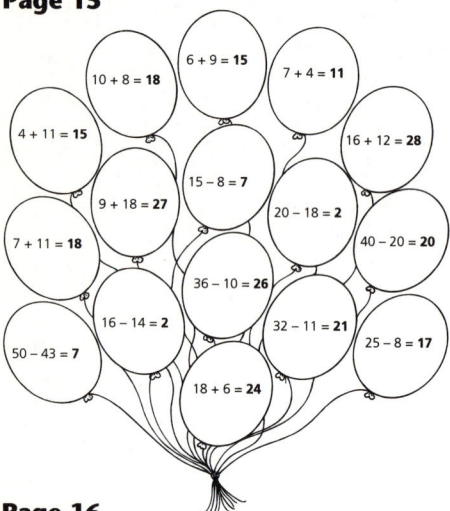

Page 16
1. animals
2. vegetables
3. numbers
4. Answers will vary.

Page 17
Answers will vary.

Page 18
1. 10, 18, 20
2. 7, 15
3. 15, 30
4. 8, 2
5. 15, 6
6. 9, 15, 15
7. 16, 24, 32
8. 21, 9, 6, 3
9. 4, 12, 12, 16, 20, 20

Page 19
Verbs: write, fix, send, bought, put, sell, fly, run, jumped, ski, slide, raced, hopped, cry

Page 20
1. 3 x 5 or 5 x 3 = 15
2. 3 x 7 or 7 x 3 = 21
3. 4 x 4 = 16
4. 3 x 2 or 2 x 3 = 6
5. 2 x 5 or 5 x 2 = 10
6. 1 x 5 or 5 x 1 = 5
7. 3 x 6 or 6 x 3 = 18
8. 4 x 5 or 5 x 4 = 20

Page 21
1. happy, glad
2. big, huge
3. sick, ill
4. evening, night
5. chore, job
6. hot, cold
7. tall, short
8. quiet, noisy
9. dark, light
10. sad, happy
11. D
12. S
13. D
14. S
15. D

Page 22
snowboot, rabbit, fish, socks, flowers, tire, book upside down, two suns

Page 23
1. square, circle, square
2. triangle, semicircle, triangle
3. circle with one dot, circle with one dot, circle with two dots
4. rectangle, diamond
5. circle, diamond, square
6. square, triangle, triangle with two dots

Page 24
1. ball, pail
2. fox, socks
3. fork, bike
4. rink, rock, sink
5. mouse, blouse
6. dish, splash

Page 25
2. table, cloth
3. sun, shine
4. dish, pan
5. class, room
6. book, case
7. tree, top
8. play, ground
9. high, way
10. sun, tan
11. camp, fire
12. birth, day
13. bed, room
14. news, paper

Page 26
Long: home, might, wild, light, take, place, scrape, bite, know, pipe
Short: hit, cut, last, bat, wash, pin, tub, black, rub, felt

Page 27
1. 1/2
2. 2/4 or 1/2
3. 3/4
4. 1/3
5. 4/6 or 2/3
6. 2/5
7. 3/3 or 1
8. 5/8

Page 28
1. 8:30
2. 10:30
3. 11:00
4. 6:15
5. 8:45
6. 4:30
7. 12:15
8. 6:45
9. 9:00
10. 7:15
11. 1:30
12. 12:00

Page 29
1. teacher/Answers will vary.
2. pilot/Answers will vary.

Page 30
1. The bedroom in my new house is painted blue.
2. Where do you go to school?
3. Do you like to take the school bus?
4. All my new friends are very nice.
5. The teacher took our class on a trip.
6. What is your favorite school subject?

Page 31
1. 6
2. 36
3. 12
4. 30
5. 18
6. 12
7. 24
8. 6
9. 30
10. 9
11. 0
12. 18

Page 32
1. 8:30 A.M.
2. 3:30 P.M.
3. 4:00 P.M., 30 minutes
4. before
5. plays with his dog
6. one hour

Page 33
1. apples
2. puppies
3. dogs
4. teacher
5. party
6. friends
7. children
8. stories
9. cat
10. ring

Page 34
2. I will
3. She would
4. We have
5. I am
6. There is
7. He would
8. They will
9. Here is
10. She will
11. He is
12. I would

Page 35
1. ounces
2. pounds
3. pounds
4. pounds
5. ounces
6. pounds
7. ounces
8. ounces
9. pounds

Page 36
1. 4 x 3 = 12
2. 2 x 3 = 6
3. 4 x 2 = 8
4. 2 x 6 = 12
5. 3 x 3 = 9

Page 37
1. We love to swim in the pool.
2. The dog jumped in the pool.
3. Hurry up and jump in!
4. Let's eat hot dogs and chips.
5. What a great day!
6. I like Maria's bathing suit.
7. Everyone is going to eat lunch.
8. Jill doesn't like to swim.
9. Swim faster, Maria!
10. This is so much fun!

Page 38
1. shut, vacation
2. rush, attention, action
3. shine, trash
4. shoulder, shake
5. show, bush, station
6. push, relation, addition
7. shun, crush, subtraction
8. clash, lotion
9. mention, fresh
10. mash, notion

Answer Key

Page 39
A. apple, everyone, return
B. camp, food, horse
C. bee, mark, special
D. like, piano, week
E. night, together, very
F. mom, never, pie

Page 40

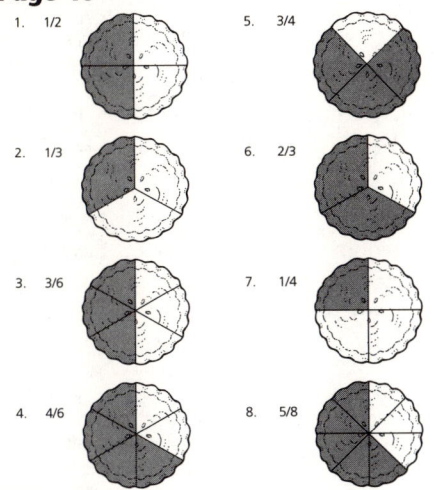

1. 1/2
2. 1/3
3. 3/6
4. 4/6
5. 3/4
6. 2/3
7. 1/4
8. 5/8

Page 41
6, 4, 2, 5, 1, 3

Page 42
Answers will vary.

Page 43
1. 16, 20
2. 16, 8, 4
3. 12, 21, 27
4. 15, 5, 5
5. 24, 18, 6, 3
6. 10, 12, 14, 16, 18
7. 25, 30, 35, 40, 45
8. 40, 30, 20, 10

Page 44
Hard "g" Sound: game, gold, gift, give, globe, girl
Soft "g" Sound: gem, geography, gingerbread, gentle, gym, giant

Page 45
1. $.40
2. $1.05
3. $2.25
4. $1.35
5. $2.20
6. $3.75
7. $.99

Page 46
1. 86 farm animals
2. 77 gallons
3. 37 postcards
4. 91 miles
5. 26 balloons

Page 47
1. in the park
2. reading
3. peanuts
4. warm
5. happy
6. frisbee

Page 48
Grocery Store: milk, apple, tomato, beans, cake
Zoo: lion, bear, tiger, elephant, monkey

Clothing Store: shoe, gloves, blouse, coat, hat
School: book, desk, teacher, student, chalk

Page 49
One-syllable words: brave, head, glass, ball, desk, but, hard, book
Two-syllable words: able, little, adult, friendly, after, table, hillside, looking, easy, tissue, middle, picture, apple
Three-syllable words: telephone, difficult, adventure, important, microphone, computer

Page 50
1. 56
2. 79
3. 109
4. 927
5. 638
6. 2,018
7. 4,446

Page 51
1. stick, pick
2. mow, row
3. drink, sink, rink
4. wrap, clap, tap
5. like, Mike
6. dig, big
7. chair, wear, care
8. dust, rust
9. top, mop
10. sing, swing, wing

Page 52
1. cats
2. parties
3. ponies
4. gifts
5. cherries
6. countries
7. books
8. bowls
9. trees
10. stories

Page 53
1. Henry lived on the big farm.
2. Henry ate breakfast.
3. They played outside.
4. Henry crossed the big field.
5. Under a big apple tree.

Page 54
1. yes
2. no
3. yes
4. yes
5. no
6. yes

Page 55
1. 0
2. 8
3. 7
4. 14
5. 6
6. 7
7. 28
8. 9
9. 4
10. 21
11. 10
12. 25
13. 3
14. 6
15. 6
16. 10
17. 10
18. 12

Page 56
1. 24
2. 30
3. 10
4. 12

Page 57
1. monkeys
2. trees
3. sun
4. mother
5. friend
6. zoo
7. koalas
8. tigers
9. giraffes, necks
10. bears
11. zebras
12. elephants, peanuts
13. snakes
14. animal, lion
15. kangaroos
16. hyenas, us
17. we, seals, fish
18. penguins, birds

Page 58

1	2	3	**4**	5	6	**7**	8	9	10
11	12	**13**	14	**15**	**16**	17	**18**	**19**	**20**
21	22	**23**	**24**	25	26	**27**	**28**	29	**30**
31	**32**	33	**34**	**35**	**36**	37	**38**	**39**	**40**
41	**42**	**43**	44	**45**	46	**47**	48	**49**	50
51	52	**53**	**54**	55	**56**	**57**	**58**	59	**60**
61	**62**	63	**64**	**65**	**66**	67	**68**	**69**	70
71	**72**	**73**	74	**75**	**76**	**77**	78	**79**	**80**
81	82	**83**	**84**	85	86	**87**	**88**	89	90
91	**92**	93	**94**	95	**96**	**97**	**98**	**99**	**100**

Page 59
1. happy
2. several, yellow
3. nice, noisy
4. big, new
5. long, red
6. cool, green
7. laughing
8. warm
9. little
10. many, fun

Page 60
1. play
2. blows
3. builds
4. knocks
5. feels
6. is collecting
7. found
8. splash
9. runs
10. is melting

Page 61
1. after
2. before
3. after
4. before
5. after
6. after

Page 62
Soft "c" Sound: cent, city, certain, cymbal, citizen, celery, circus, cinder
Hard "c" Sound: curtain, come, cone, comb, cook, call, color, camp

Page 63
ant, apple, cent, clap, deer, dirt, down, goat, take, tent, were, where

Page 64

101	102	103	**104**	**105**	106	107	**108**	**109**	110
111	112	**113**	114	115	**116**	**117**	118	119	120
121	**122**	123	**124**	125	**126**	127	**128**	129	**130**
131	**132**	**133**	134	**135**	136	**137**	138	**139**	140
141	142	143	**144**	145	**146**	**147**	148	149	**150**
151	**152**	**153**	154	**155**	156	157	**158**	**159**	160
161	162	**163**	**164**	165	166	**167**	168	169	**170**
171	**172**	173	**174**	175	**176**	177	**178**	**179**	180
181	182	**183**	**184**	185	186	**187**	188	189	**190**
191	**192**	193	**194**	195	**196**	197	**198**	**199**	200

Answer Key

Page 65
1. 75 balloons   2. 89 points
3. $2.85   4. 51 tickets
5. $3.25

Page 66
1. 11:00 A.M.   2. 6:00 P.M.
3. 4:30 P.M.   4. 4:00 A.M.
5. 8:00 A.M.   6. 6:30 A.M.
7. 7:30 P.M.   8. 9:00 P.M.
9. 10:30 A.M.   10. 10:00 P.M.

Page 67
1. plane   2. train   3. friend
4. tree   5. flower   6. drive
7. swing   8. clap   9. traffic
10. plate

Page 69
Two-syllable words: doc/tor, home/made, cor/ner, tea/cher, pen/cil, buy/ing, play/ground, ac/tion, ad/dress, cam/el
Three-syllable words: his/to/ry, cal/cu/late, re/la/tive, time/ta/ble, beau/ti/ful, de/co/rate, jus/ti/fy, per/mis/sion, af/ter/noon, bas/ket/ball

Page 70
1. 146   2. 480   3. 697
4. 918   5. 725   6. 255
7. 330   8. 111   9. 503
10. 809   11. 237   12. 189
13. 371   14. 523   15. 975
16. 133

Page 71
Capitalized: Thanksgiving, Tuesday, Texas, September, Christmas, October, Susie, New York
Not Capitalized: monkey, valentine, hot dog, elm, fruit, microphone, turkey, mother

Page 72
A. 9, 16, 24, 26   B. 67, 56, 62, 16
C. 46, 39, 32, 38   D. 49, 59, 39, 46

Page 73
1. It's the school art fair.
2. They are helping at the third-grade booth.
3. Thomas made a sailboat out of wood.
4. Anna made a necklace from seashells.
5. They will visit other booths at the fair.

Page 74
1. 8:05   2. 6:15   3. 7:20
4. 10:35   5. 2:10   6. 8:25
7. 11:55   8. 12:50   9. 10:40

Page 75
1. 44 visitors   2. 39 books
3. 64 children   4. 144 books
5. 12 days

Page 76
2. helped, past   3. planned, past
4. study, present   5. talks, present
6. answers, present   7. sat, past
8. laughed, past   9. receives, present
10. want, present

Page 77
Common Nouns: girl, ocean, blouse, birthday, friend, vegetable, street, sister
Proper Nouns: Oak Avenue, Anna, Smith Bakery, New York, Frank Jones, Uncle Joe, December, Tuesday

Page 78
1. three   2. seven   3. Panthers
4. Tigers   5. more   6. ten

Page 79
2. Will we leave for our vacation on August 3, 1997?
3. My older brother was twelve on April 11, 1997.
4. José's tenth birthday is on February 2, 1998.
5. Someday I would love to visit Washington, D.C.
6. My best friend is from New York, New York.
7. Did Mr. Morgan travel to Portland, Oregon last summer?
8. Can we visit an art museum in Los Angeles, California?

Page 80
A. 50, 18, 71, 64   B. 83, 76, 60, 19
C. 42, 52, 26, 31   D. 64, 23, 82, 38

Page 81
1. Molly's
2. dog's
3. Mr. Green's
4. mother's, night's
5. boy's, Henry's
6. swimmer's, ocean's
7. Maria's, dog's

Page 82
2. one hundred, six tens, five ones
3. two hundreds, nine tens, four ones
4. three hundreds, one ten, six ones
5. nine hundreds, six tens, four ones
6. six hundreds, one ten, two ones
7. five hundreds, three tens, seven ones
8. eight hundreds, two tens, zero ones

Page 83
Words with silent "e": bite, shake, gate, plane, note, pole, mile, huge, freeze

Page 84
1. $4.05   2. $1.93   3. $4.44
4. $.15   5. $.39

Page 85
1. 31   2. 19   3. 55
4. 97   5. 45   6. 56
7. 76   8. 60   9. 30
10. 40
1. 7   2. 28   3. 80
4. 18   5. 44   6. 73
7. 98   8. 12   9. 39
10. 78   11. 25   12. 50
13. 22   14. 89

Page 86
1. eight   2. rose   3. bear
4. wood   5. sun   6. flower
7. deer

Page 87

Page 88

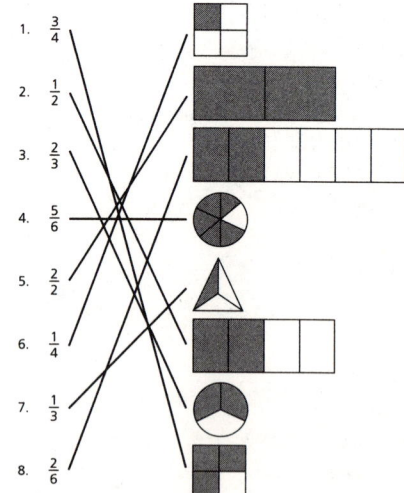

Page 92
1. >   2. <   3. <
4. <   5. >   6. >
7. <   8. >   9. <
10. <   11. >   12. <
13. >   14. >   15. >
16. >   17. >   18. >

Assessment Overview

Thinking about Assessment

As a student, your child will encounter both teacher-made and standardized tests. These tests will be in a variety of formats, including multiple choice, fill-in-the-blanks, true or false, and matching. It's important to ensure that your child is familiar with different testing formats and comfortable in a testing situation.

How to Use the Tests

The pretest and posttests included in this book can be used to assess your child's level of understanding both before and after completing the activities. The tests focus on the same language arts and math skills that are reinforced in the book and familiarize students with some common testing formats.

Keep the following tips in mind before giving the tests:

- Talk to your child about each test. Explain its purpose and briefly review its content.
- Encourage your child to discuss his or her feelings about taking tests. Help your child develop a positive attitude about testing.
- Tell your child that he or she may skip a question if it is too difficult, but that it is important to try to complete the entire test. If your child has trouble with a particular concept, he or she can practice the skill by completing the activities in the book.
- Help your child create a good testing environment. Testing should take place in a quiet area, away from distractions such as games, electronic equipment, or other children. Provide a supply of sharpened pencils and an eraser.

Sight Words

The following list of sight words includes vocabulary that students should be able to read and write by the end of second grade. Copy these words on 3" x 5" cards and use them to test your child. Also encourage him or her to make up sentences for the words or use several of the words in an original story.

able	engine	nail
above	eye	nice
across	fair	number
afraid	fence	outside
ahead	front	oven
almost	frog	own
anyone	glass	part
ate	glove	path
basketball	got	pile
beautiful	happen	policeman
been	help	push
believe	hope	quack
blew	hungry	quickly
both	idea	raccoon
branch	important	railroad
cage	isn't	sad
candy	joke	same
caught	jolly	save
climb	keep	soft
clothes	lady	table
dear	lock	true
didn't	machine	us
donkey	mice	use
easy	minute	very
eight	moon	village

Pretest

Multiple choice questions are made up of a question or a sentence and answer choices. Try to think of an answer before looking at the choices. Then find the choice that matches your answer.

Example: What word means the same as happy?

○ sad   ○ glad   ○ red

Answer: ○ glad

Read each question and the choices. Then fill in the circle to show the correct answer.

1. Which word means the same as *big*?

    ○ large   ○ small   ○ tiny

2. Which word means the opposite of *sunny*?

    ○ wet   ○ long   ○ cloudy

3. Which word means the same as *wonderful*?

    ○ live   ○ try   ○ great

4. Which word means the opposite of *easy*?

    ○ difficult   ○ fast   ○ jolly

5. Which word means the same as *silly*?

    ○ dark   ○ funny   ○ girl

6. Which word means the opposite of *quickly*?

    ○ sadly   ○ very   ○ slowly

Pretest

Multiple choice problems can also be math problems. Read each problem. Then fill in the circle next to the correct answer.

1. 30 − 12 = ____   ○ 12   ○ 6   ○ 18

2. 4 x 7 = ____   ○ 11   ○ 28   ○ 32

3. ▭ ○ ▭ ○ ____

   ○ ○   ○ ▭   ○ △

4. 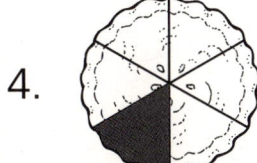   ○ 5/6   ○ 1/2   ○ 7/8

5. [clock]   ○ 5:30   ○ 3:30   ○ 2:30

6. 15 __ 5 = 20   ○ +   ○ −   ○ ×

7.

   ○ $3.00   ○ $3.52   ○ $2.50

8. 52
   − 28
   _____   ○ 30   ○ 60   ○ 24

9. 6 __ 6 = 36   ○ ×   ○ +   ○ −

© Frank Schaffer Publications, Inc.   FS-23404 Summer Skills for the 2nd Grade Graduate

Pretest

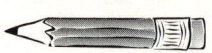

Fill in the circle next to the sentence that has the correct punctuation.

1. ○ max and maria played on the beach
   ○ Max and maria played on the beach
   ○ Max and Maria played on the beach.

2. ○ Marias beach bag is red and blue.
   ○ Maria's beach bag is red and blue.
   ○ marias' beach bag is red and blue?

3. ○ We last visited the beach on July 4, 1999.
   ○ We last visited the beach on july 4 1999
   ○ we last visited the beach on july 4, 1999

4. ○ Can we visit another beach in Ocean Park New Jersey
   ○ can we visit another beach in ocean park new jersey
   ○ Can we visit another beach in Ocean Park, New Jersey?

Read each problem carefully. Then write the correct answer on the blank line.

5. Sam bought 3 books. Sue bought 8 books. Altogether, Sam and Sue bought _____ books.

6. Jimmy had 50 cents. He bought a pencil for 20 cents. Then he bought an eraser for 10 cents. Jimmy had _____ cents left.

7. Ms. Garcia bought 18 ounces of chopped meat. She bought 32 ounces of chicken. Altogether, Ms. Garcia bought _____ ounces of chopped meat and chicken.

8. Howard spent $2.50 for milk and $1.50 for cheese. Then, Ellen spent $6.00 for vegetables. Howard and Ellen spent _____ for milk, cheese, and vegetables.

Posttest

 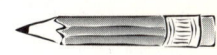

Read each sentence. Look at the **bold** word. Is it a noun, a verb, or an adjective? Fill in the circle to show the correct answer.

1. There are **many** children at the playground today.
   ○ noun   ○ verb   ○ adjective

2. Soon a **clown** will put on a show for us.
   ○ noun   ○ verb   ○ adjective

3. This new **playground** has many swings and slides.
   ○ noun   ○ verb   ○ adjective

4. The children **ran** in the grass all day long.
   ○ noun   ○ verb   ○ adjective

Read each sentence. There is one word missing. Is it a noun that means one, or that means more than one? Fill in the blank in the sentence with a word from the word box.

blouse   blouses   dog   dogs   lady   ladies   party   parties   pony   ponies

5. There are three _____ barking in our yard.

6. I like to ride both _____ at the zoo.

7. Two _____ are on a bench waiting for a bus.

8. I will buy one new _____ to wear to school.

9. Sue and Max went to two birthday _____ this weekend.

Posttest

A. Add or subtract. Then fill in the circle to show the correct answer.

1. 14
   + 22   ○ 36   ○ 60   ○ 42

2. 15
   + 37   ○ 30   ○ 52   ○ 43

3. 150
   − 128   ○ 32   ○ 22   ○ 18

4. 186
   + 263   ○ 348   ○ 503   ○ 449

5. 308
   − 247   ○ 61   ○ 101   ○ 72

B. Multiply. Then fill in the circle to show the correct answer.

6. 6 x 4 =   ○ 20   ○ 12   ○ 24

7. 7 x 2 =   ○ 30   ○ 14   ○ 28

8. 10 x 4 =   ○ 20   ○ 30   ○ 40

9. 8 x 4 =   ○ 32   ○ 24   ○ 8

10. 3 x 9 =   ○ 36   ○ 6   ○ 27

Posttest

Fill in the blank in each sentence with the right word from the word box.

laughs	paints	washed	sang	planted

1. Lee _____ his dirty dog in the bathtub.

2. Everyone _____ at the funny clown in the play.

3. Yesterday all the children _____ a song in class.

4. Today, Maria _____ a picture of her two dogs.

5. Last week my dad and I _____ flowers in the yard.

Read each problem. Fill in the circle next to the correct answer.

6. There are 12 apples in Sue's basket. She gave 9 apples to Ellen. How many apples did Sue have left?
    - ○ 4
    - ○ 5
    - ○ 3

7. Louis has 18 crayons in his box. Julie has 7 crayons in her box. How many crayons do they have altogether?
    - ○ 25
    - ○ 29
    - ○ 15

8. There are 6 cars in the train. There are 5 people in each car. How many people are in the train altogether?
    - ○ 18
    - ○ 30
    - ○ 20

9. There are 8 boxes in the grocery store. There are 7 cans in each box. How many cans are in the boxes?
    - ○ 56
    - ○ 48
    - ○ 16

Answers

Beginning-of-Summer Pretest

Page 98
1. large
2. cloudy
3. great
4. difficult
5. funny
6. slowly

Page 99
1. 18
2. 28
3. rectangle
4. 5/6
5. 3:30
6. minus (–)
7. $3.52
8. 24
9. times (x)

Page 100
1. third sentence
2. second sentence
3. first sentence
4. third sentence
5. 11
6. 20
7. 50
8. $10.00

End-of-Summer Posttest

Page 101
1. adjective
2. noun
3. noun
4. verb
5. dogs
6. ponies
7. ladies
8. blouse
9. parties

Page 102
1. 36
2. 52
3. 22
4. 449
5. 61
6. 24
7. 14
8. 40
9. 32
10. 27

Page 103
1. washed
2. laughs
3. sang
4. paints
5. planted
6. 3
7. 25
8. 30
9. 56

stop, slot

____ + ____ = baseball

boat, tote

____ + ____ = breakfast

laugh, strap, bad

____ + ____ = starfish

stay, braid

____ + ____ = bedroom

fell, step

____ + ____ = eyeball

street, leaf

____ + ____ = playpen

trip, mix

____ + ____ = shoelace

stripe, kind

____ + ____ = peanut

under, ugly, udder

____ + ____ = cowboy

universe, use

____ + ____ = rainbow

© Frank Schaffer Publications, Inc.

FS-23404 Summer Skills for the 2nd Grade Graduate

break, fast	base, ball
Long o	**Short o**
boat, cot, long, tote	shout, stop, slot, coat

bed, room	star, fish
Long a	**Short a**
stay, sad, braid, apple	laugh, strap, cape, bad

play, pen	eye, ball
Long e	**Short e**
street, leaf, tell, shell	feel, fell, tree, step

pea, nut	shoe, lace
Long i	**Short i**
stripe, strip, clip, kind	mind, trip, mix, like

rain, bow	cow, boy
Long u	**Short u**
universe, bump, mumps, use	under, unicorn, ugly, udder

© Frank Schaffer Publications, Inc.

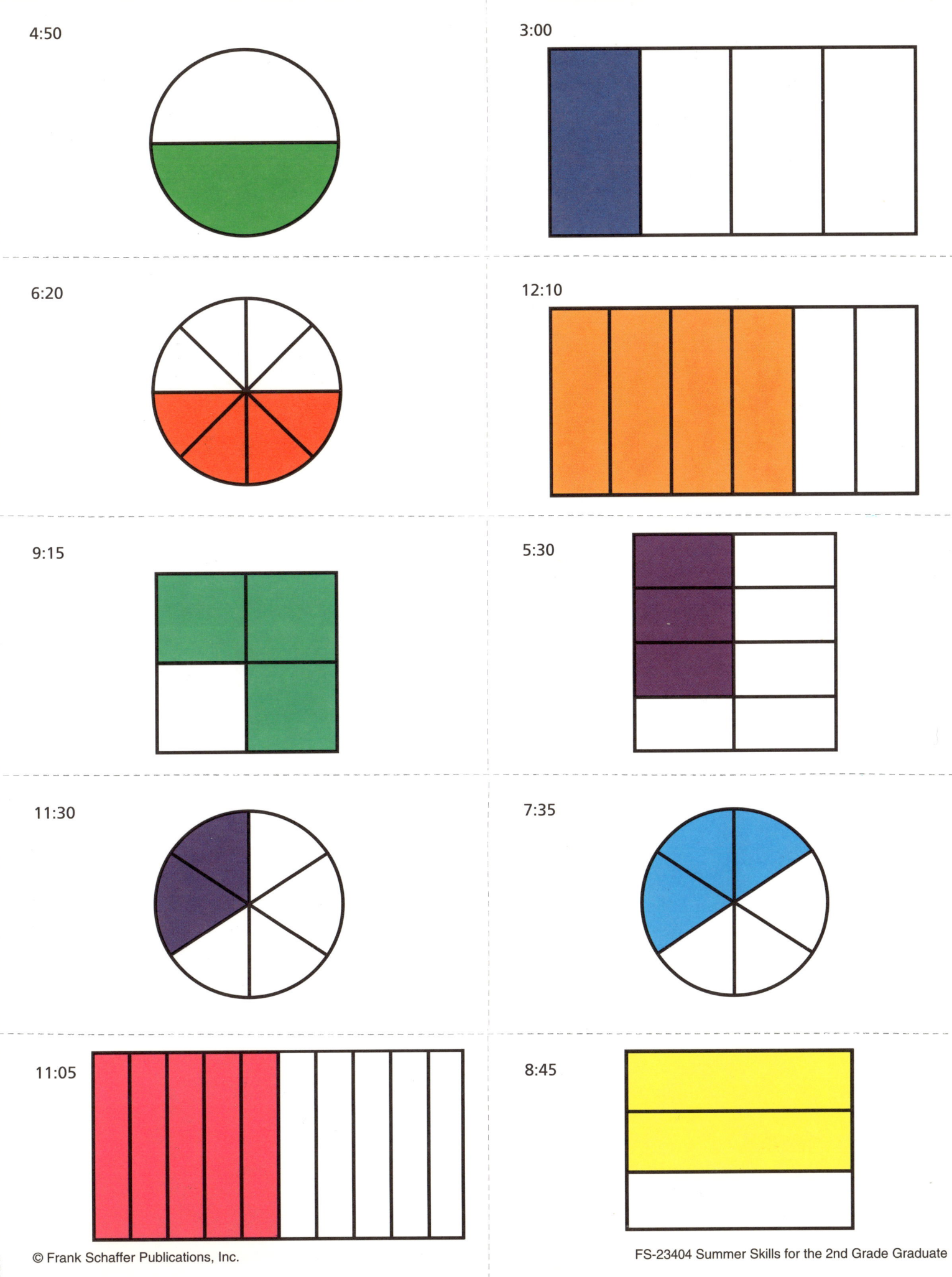

¼  ½

4/6 or 2/3  4/8 or ½

3/8  ¾

3/6 or ½  2/6 or 1/3

2/3  5/10 or ½

© Frank Schaffer Publications, Inc.   FS-23404 Summer Skills for the 2nd Grade Graduate

15	3
3 + 7	**1 + 9**

4	3
11 + 15	**7 + 7**

7	17
8 + 8	**6 + 8**

8	11
10 + 30	**10 + 10**

9	10
12 + 7	**18 + 3**

© Frank Schaffer Publications, Inc.   FS-23404 Summer Skills for the 2nd Grade Graduate

10	10
10 − 7	**20 − 5**

14	26
11 − 8	**13 − 9**

14	16
25 − 8	**16 − 9**

20	40
18 − 7	**20 − 12**

21	19
19 − 9	**17 − 8**

© Frank Schaffer Publications, Inc.

8 1 x 1	9 2 x 2
7 3 x 3	6 4 x 4
6 5 x 5	4 6 x 6
8 7 x 7	2 8 x 8
9 9 x 9	5 10 x 10

4	1
54 ÷ 6	**40 ÷ 5**

16	9
42 ÷ 7	**56 ÷ 8**

36	25
24 ÷ 6	**36 ÷ 6**

64	49
20 ÷ 10	**32 ÷ 4**

100	81
45 ÷ 9	**72 ÷ 8**

© Frank Schaffer Publications, Inc.

Numbers 1-100

1	2	3	4	5	6	7	8	9	10
11	12	13	14	15	16	17	18	19	20
21	22	23	24	25	26	27	28	29	30
31	32	33	34	35	36	37	38	39	40
41	42	43	44	45	46	47	48	49	50
51	52	53	54	55	56	57	58	59	60
61	62	63	64	65	66	67	68	69	70
71	72	73	74	75	76	77	78	79	80
81	82	83	84	85	86	87	88	89	90
91	92	93	94	95	96	97	98	99	100

© Frank Schaffer Publications, Inc.

FS-23404 Summer Skills for the Second Grade Graduate